The Man who Chopped History in Half

The Man
Who Chopped History
In Half

Frank Pagden

EPWORTH PRESS

British Library Cataloguing in Publication Data
Pagden, Frank
    The man who chopped history in half.
    1. Jesus Christ
    I. Title
    232

    ISBN 0–7162–0461–4

First published 1989 by
Epworth Press
Room 195, 1 Central Buildings, Westminster
London SW1H 9NR

Phototypeset by J&L Composition Ltd,
Filey, North Yorkshire
and printed in Great Britain by
Richard Clay Ltd, Bungay, Suffolk

Contents

v

To Local Radio Pilgrims
and 'God Squads'
with gratitude

Introduction

It was as if I had spent a lazy afternoon wandering round a town that I used to know fairly well, and was revisiting, to find to my surprise little courts and byways that I never knew were there – parks which I had rushed by in previous years; cobbled squares of Georgian shops which had been hidden from me by the supermarket, mounting stones still set on the roadside; Victorian alley-ways which time had left untouched. In my previous familiarity with the town I had prided myself that I knew it pretty well, but I now realized that I had known only the main roads, and in the process of using them I had missed its character; had been too busy to notice its 'feel'.

This book is the result of a revisiting like that. In past years I thought I knew what Jesus was like – as much as any ordinary person could. The Sunday School cardboard cut-out with which I grew up had been enlarged and filled out by reading the New Testament and background books, until at last I felt I knew the main outlines of the ministry, passion and death of this extraordinary person.

Then a little while ago I helped to lead a pilgrimage of 242 Yorkshire people to the Holy Land. This was followed by two other opportunities to visit that country of which it is said that it has too much history and not enough geography. The sight of the context of Jesus, and the necessary study which had to be done made me realize that he was much more extraordinary than I had thought. I may have known the main roads, but I had entirely missed the atmosphere of the historical Jesus. Bobbing on the Lake of Galilee in a boat, dabbling in the River Jordan, walking the dusty slopes of the Kidron Valley, and soaking in the quiet of the Garden of Gethsemane, added a reality to my imaginary picture of him, and changed much of it. Many questions arose in my mind when I returned home, my curiosity was roused, and I set to work re-reading the Gospels. I started with St Mark's Gospel, reasoning that as the earliest, possibly written from St Peter's preaching material, there might be unmistakable eye-witness touches which had survived thirty years of sermons and St Mark's memory.

For instance, the only story from the teaching ministry of Jesus which appears in all four Gospels is the Feeding of the Five Thousand (an interesting puzzle in itself, why only that one?). Of the four different versions of the story, Mark's is the only one which says that Jesus commanded the people to sit down 'on the green grass'. This may seem nothing to us in England, where the grass is always that colour, but in Palestine the grass is *not* always green, for much of the year it is brown. So when Peter tells, and Mark records the grass as green, he is pinning down the story to the spring-time, and we can deduce that it was about 6 pm in April. When Mark describes the people sitting down in groups he uses a gardening term saying that they looked like 'rows of vegetables'. This could only have come from someone who was there.

These little eye-witness touches do not effect the story at all, but perhaps there were others which could shed unexpected gleams of light on the character of Jesus, to tell us more of what he was like. Following this up I found that Mark wasn't the only source of these sparkling little details, they could be found in the other Gospels too. To return to the Feeding of the Five Thousand – Matthew, Mark and Luke tell the story in very similar ways, but John is different. The charm of the story for many people is the picture of the lad whose mother had packed in his lunch box the crucial five barley loaves and two fishes which were the starting point of the miracle. He is only mentioned by John, probably the latest of the Gospel writers, who is also the only one to tell us which of the disciples were there – that inseparable pair of 'buddies', the modest Philip and the good-natured Andrew. It is as if when the Gospel of St John was written, the writer had before him the other three and said 'ah, but we know who was there, because he told us!'

So, from looking at the ancient sites in Israel, re-reading the New Testament with fresh eyes, and trying to match the one with the other, I found things about Jesus that were to me at least, unusual and exciting.

Of course, I recognize that I am 'reading between the lines' rather more than some scholars might say is proper. Experts in biblical studies and archaeology are rightly very careful and cautious about their conclusions, as authorities on the subjects they have to test every link in every chain of evidence and reasoning. That is only proper in their field, and we wouldn't think much of them if they didn't. However, this isn't that kind of book, and in this account I have made many assumptions. I have, however, done this on what evidence I have found, and tried to be fair; when a conclusion is not academically proved, I have liberally sprinkled words like 'possible', 'probable', and 'perhaps'. This account is designed especially for the non-expert, but for those who wish to follow up any of the subjects mentioned there are, of course, many scholarly books available.

The search for the Jesus his friends and relatives knew is a traditional one, and flourished in the nineteenth century. In general the quest was not very successful, swinging this way and that. At some times scholars seemed to have found new things about him, compiling great 'Lives of Christ' which justified their own theories, and at other times they almost despaired of ever discovering anything at all about the historical Jesus. A generation or two ago extreme scepticism was the fashion, and I can remember speakers who would have had difficulty writing what they thought was genuine from the Gospels on to one side of a sheet of paper. Now the pendulum is swinging back, and we are finding even with the most modern of historical tools and archaeological techniques that the Jesus of history is impervious to the most rigorous of investigations. In short, this fascinating character just refuses to go away.

But however clever and diligent the study, and whatever surprising bits of knowledge turn up, we are always faced with an infuriating fog over what the Jesus of the first century was like. We know more about him from the Gospels – a lot more than about any other person of that period – yet we don't know enough to bring him into focus. For the Gospels are not biographies, they tell us nothing at all about what he looked like or was like. Everything about him has to be tentatively drawn out from incidental references in the stories of what he said and did. The Gospel writers were writing Gospels, not life-stories – documents to persuade, rather than to inform for interest's sake.

One is also tempted to forget that for periods during the first three hundred years Christianity was discouraged, persecuted, and driven underground. Christian buildings were demolished, Christian books burned, and crucial eye-witnesses dispersed and harried. The result is that before the installation of Constantine as the first Christian

Roman Emperor there is very little archaeological evidence to be seen in Palestine, or elsewhere for that matter. There is a sense in which the first century Jesus must always be much of a mystery.

Albert Schweitzer was right when he wrote:
He comes to us as One unknown, without a name, as of old, by the lakeside. He came to those men who knew Him not. He speaks to us the same word: 'Follow thou me!' and sets us to the tasks which He has to fulfil for our time. He commands. And to those who obey Him, whether they be wise or simple, he will reveal himself in the toils, the conflicts, the sufferings which they shall pass through in His fellowship, and as an ineffable mystery, they shall learn in their own experience *Who He* is.

This is the Christ of Faith, whom we shall consider at the end of the book, and who only can make sensible and valid the first-century Jesus. Yet it is precisely a live awareness of the Jesus of Faith that enhances our interest in what he was like when he lived in Palestine two thousand years ago. That's why we want to know about him.

It is often said that Jesus was the most influential man who ever lived. Yet he never commanded an army, never ruled a country, never fought a battle, never painted a picture, and never even wrote a book. His impact on the economics, politics, and culture of his country while he was alive was exactly nil! It is a quite astounding thing. What was his secret? What was he like? I suppose that everyone has their own individual answer to that question, and that there are as many different pictures as there are people. My hope, in looking sideways through the cracks in the Gospel narratives, and catching occasional glimpses through accidental openings in the stories and the historical remains, is that our rough outline may be filled out a little and deepened.

1

The Divine One-Off

What was Jesus like?

So Joseph woke from sleep, and did as the angel of the
Lord had commanded him; and accepted his wife . . .
and she bore a son and he called his name Jesus.

His name was YESHWA in Hebrew, often anglicized as
JOSHUA, in the family's native language of Aramaic it was
YESHU'A. Reading from right to left the letters are: Yod,
Shin, Vaw, and the unpronounceable 'Ain. The first letter
Yod, is the smallest in the Hebrew alphabet, from which
we get our word 'jot'. The Greeks called him YEH-ZOOS,
from which the Romans got JESU, and we get the English
JESUS. As a person Jesus may have been unique, but
there was nothing unusual about the name at all, plenty
of people in Old Testament times, and in first-century
Palestine bore it.

For example, a century and a half BC, there was a
notorious Jesus, who after being made High Priest, was
deposed, and after changing his name to the Greek style of
Jason, raised a successful rebellion. Another Jesus, the son
of Ananus a peasant farmer, about 61 AD became well-
known in Jerusalem for being mad, in so far as he spent no
less than seven years wandering round the city day and
night disrupting worship and sleepers alike by shouting

'woe, woe to Jerusalem.' He did it once too often on the walls of Jerusalem during the Roman seige, and was killed by a high-velocity Roman boulder. One Jesus, son of Sapphias the high-priest, was elected a general to fight the Romans during the Jewish Wars, then there was Jesus the son of Saphat, who was ringleader of a band of robbers – and those are just the well-known ones, there were so many more. Ironically, an early manuscript of the Gospels from Caesarea gives the first name of Barabbas, the robber who was freed in preference to Jesus on the night before the Crucifixion, as JESUS Barabbas. Pilate could have asked the crowd to choose between two Jesus's – Jesus Barjoseph and Jesus Barabbas. So it is quite clear that there was nothing special about the name JESUS.

What did he look like? The brutal fact is that nobody knows. For Jewish religious reasons, no painted portraits or sculptured busts were ever made of any Jew, let alone of Jesus, during his lifetime. In the Syrian Convent of St Mark in Jerusalem they proudly show to visitors a picture of Mary the mother of Jesus, which they say was actually painted on leather by Luke. As a Gentile Luke (or to give him his full Latin name, Lucanus) was just the person who might have painted one, but the painting cannot be dated before about 500 AD, so isn't authentic, and indeed there is another similar painting also claiming to be by Luke in a Spanish cathedral. As there is a strong early tradition that Luke was a skilled painter, are we likely to discover a Lukan portrait of Jesus anywhere? It's most unlikely, because as far as we can tell Luke never saw him in the flesh, and came into the church after the resurrection. He probably did see Mary, for reasons we shall look at in a later chapter.

What is more surprising is that we have no written accounts of what Jesus looked like. No descriptions of his appearance were written by the disciples, much to our loss, or if they were, they have not survived; the pen-portraits in later Christian books cannot be relied on, they are pure products of the pious imagination.

For instance, one clear forgery purports to be a letter written to the Roman Senate by Lentulus, who was in Judaea at the time, in which he says:

> He is tall of stature, and his aspect is sweet and full of power, so that they who look upon him may at once love and fear him. The hair of his head is the colour of wine; as far as the ears it is straight and without glitter, from the ears to the shoulders it is curled and glossy, and from the shoulders it descends over the back, divided into two parts, after the manner of the Nazarenes. His brow is pure and even; his countenance without a spot, but adorned with a gentle glow; his expression bland and open; his nose and mouth are of perfect beauty; his beard is copious, forked, and of the colour of his hair; his eyes are blue and very bright. In reproving and threatening he is terrible, in teaching and exhorting gentle and loving. The grace and majesty of his appearance are marvellous. No one has ever seen him laugh, but rather weeping. His carriage is erect; his hands well formed and straight; his arms of passing beauty . . .

This letter appeared at least three centuries later, and says more about the devotions of the time than about Jesus. None of the memories of those who really remembered what he looked like have survived in any way that is credible; all we have is pious invention.

Yet imaginary as it is, we all have a mental picture of him, and over the ages this picture has changed according to how the Christian view of him and the world has developed.

The Greek idea of the gods was of people who were perfection in physical form; of god-like beauty. To the early Christian preachers of the first three centuries this was entirely wrong, and they proclaimed that the real beauty of the god-head was in a perfection of truth and morality. The result was that they often referred to Jesus as 'undistinguished' and 'inglorious', and almost all the very earliest descriptions play down any attractiveness in Jesus the man. The prophecies of Isaiah about the 'Suffering Servant of god' came in very useful for them:

He had no beauty or majesty to attract us to him,
nothing in his appearance that we should desire him.
He was despised and rejected of men . . .
Like one from whom men hide their faces
he was despised, and we esteemed him not.

It was the Greek church which most fostered the idea of a deformed Jesus; Cyril of Alexandria confidently declared that 'he was the ugliest of men'.

If we ask the question 'What did he look like?' not 'What should he have looked like?' this picture of a repulsively ugly Jesus is difficult to accept. The evidence is against it, for in the Gospel stories there are many examples of people flocking to him, individuals attracted to him, and crowds following him. The moving story of the woman of Samaria shows how a complete stranger, even one of a different race and religion, could find in this unknown Jewish man a quality of openness and approach-ability so compelling that she could ignore the traditional hostility between their races and pour out her heart and her troubles to him. And then there was the acid test – the children.

They brought little children to Jesus that he might touch them. But the disciples rebuked them. When Jesus saw what they were doing he was vexed and said to them 'Let the little children come to me, and don't try to stop them for of such is the kingdom of God'.

It was the Jewish custom in those days that mothers should bring their children at one year old to be blessed by a respected and revered Rabbi. At that age, as every parent knows, they are particularly sensitive to strangers, so it is hardly likely that they should choose to bring them to anyone who was likely to frighten them, or whose appearance they would not like.

Again, after being out on a preaching trip Jesus returned to 'the House'. Whose house? It could have been Matthew's, but my guess is that it was the home of Peter and Andrew. While there Jesus took a child – if it was Peter's house, it could have been Peter's son or his nephew, for Peter, Andrew, mother-in-law, and all the relatives lived together in quite a large house, which has recently been excavated.

> He took a little child and had him stand among them. Taking him in his arms he said to them, 'whoever welcomes one of these little children in my name, welcomes me.'

It sounds as if Jesus was very familiar with dandling children on his knee and talking to them. After all, as we shall see later, Jesus was almost certainly an uncle! There was probably a small tribe of little children in Nazareth who were always eager to hear news of what their exciting Uncle Jesus was up to. No, however right the theology was, we cannot accept an unattractive Jesus.

Neither, in the end, could the Early Church, for after the Third Century there came a swing of the pendulum, and we find Jerome (342–420) holed out at the Church of the Nativity in Bethlehem writing: 'Had he not something heavenly also in his face and in his eyes, the apostles would never have followed him at once, nor would those who had come to arrest him have fallen to the ground.' So it stayed until the seventh and eighth centuries, when more

Christian authors started to compose detailed descriptions of what he looked like, all of them claiming to be genuine, yet none of them based on any real evidence at all.

When we turn to art, Christian painters, freed from the Jewish prohibition against painting and sculpture, in the first two centuries began to exercise their own imaginations. Having no inconvenient facts to disrupt their ideas, they naturally reflected the art and the theology of the time in which they lived. Pagan converts, used to worshipping gods who were carefully carved and richly coloured, accepted that their new God was invisible and could only be worshipped 'in spirit and in truth', but nevertheless they hankered for something to look at. The first surviving pictures of Jesus show this influence – here is Jesus in the guise of a Greek god. The first Christian representations of him, like the many examples in the catacombs of Rome, show him as an idealized and beautiful beardless youth.

When Christianity became the official religion of the Roman Empire after the Emperor Constantine, it was no longer the natural faith of the poor, oppressed, and hunted. It suddenly became the patron of the powerful and the triumphant religion of the known world. So the beardless youth was overtaken by the picture of Jesus as the King of Kings. He is depicted from then on as seated on a kingly throne, surrounded by obedient subjects and given the halo of divinity round his head, a convention that up to then had only been used for Roman emperors.

In addition to the sudden change in Christian status, more and more intellectuals had been drawn to the faith over the years, and the fascination of Jesus' 'world-view' had begun to work its magic on the minds of men. So another picture of Jesus began to evolve, that of the master of thought and truth. A much more venerable picture was needed to satisfy this idea, and so we see developing a Jesus who is himself a thinker, a middle-aged man with a high forehead, a curly beard, and great dignity. This imaginary picture has been so influential that it still has a profound effect on Christian art today. In the classic Holman Hunt picture of Jesus standing outside the door of the human heart, he is shown as the perceptive man who knows.

Then in the eleventh century the Northern European gift for ornamental and abstract patterns began to affect the portraits, and the pictures were aimed at producing an abstract idea of Jesus, rather than any attempt to portray a human likeness, so we get a flat, stylized Jesus with no perspective. After that, the rise of the nation-state and protestantism emphasized the importance and the sacredness of the individual, and this more democratic age produced a more down-to-earth and human Jesus. Various artists painted him looking very vulnerable in realistic situations, and the most terrifying pictures of the crucifixion come from this time.

However, all these pictures are true and not true. Each says something true about the significance of Jesus, but all are entirely imaginary. No one knows what Jesus looked like. All one can really say with any confidence is that he looked like a first-century Middle Eastern Jew.

So what did they look like? Again, shortage of paintings and sculptures of this period make it difficult to say. If we can suppose that the physical types in that area now, were much the same then, this would indicate that Jesus was of medium height, with a sallow complexion, wiry, strong, dark-haired, and bearded, but nothing more detailed than that.

There is one intriguing possibility. In the well-known story of Zacchaeus who climbed the tree in Jericho to see Jesus go by we are told it was because he was short. Who was short – Zacchaeus or Jesus? The story can be read both ways.

So much for what he looked like, but what was he like as a person? Here we are on much more fruitful ground for we have four books of stories about him to delve into. The one certain thing is that it is impossible to stick a label on him. He was alarmingly unconventional, the ultimate in non-conformists. No one could possibly have invented him.

For one thing he was a very tough individual, both with himself and with others. He had a moral courage that came from a clear aim, and a thoroughly dedicated mind. We have already seen from Jerome that he faced down the Roman soldiers who were sent to arrest him in the Garden of Gethsemane; in the face of his moral authority and presence 'they stepped back and fell on the ground'. It was a repeat of the time when he had to face a murderous crowd in his home town of Nazareth, who took exception to his preaching:

> They rose up and hustled him out of the town. They took him to the brow of the hill on which their town is built, to throw him down; but he passed through the midst of them and went upon his way.

What an off-hand way to put it – 'he passed through the midst of them!' It reminds us inescapably of others who have faced similar perils with the same courage. Fortunately they have not been so reticent as Luke in telling us about it. When John Wesley visited Falmouth on 4 July 1745 he had not been visiting a sick lady ten minutes before:

> The house was beset on all sides by a innumerable multitude of people. The rabble roared with all their throats 'Bring out the Canorum!' (a word which the Cornish use instead of Methodist). They forced open the outer door, and filled the passage, only the wainscot

partition being between us. Poor Kitty was utterly astonished and cried out 'O Sir, what must we do?' I said 'we must pray.' Among those without were the crews of some privateers, which had lately come into the harbour. Some of these set their shoulders together at the inner door crying 'Avast, lads, avast!' Away went all the hinges at once, and the door fell back into the room.

I stepped forward at once into the midst of them and said 'here I am. Which of you has anything to say to me? To which of you have I done any wrong? To you? Or you? Or you?' I continued speaking till I came, bareheaded as I was, (for I purposely left my hat that they all might see my face), into the middle of the street, and then raising my voice said, 'neighbours, countrymen! Do you desire to hear me speak?' They cried vehemently, 'yes, yes'. I spoke without intermission . . .

It took cold-blooded moral courage to look one's enemies straight in the eye and do what Wesley did on that day. Where Jesus did it, no one quite knows. Near Nazareth there is a steep hill called the Hill of Precipitation which is the traditional site, and its cliffs could well have been a place of execution. It is, however, a fair walk from the town. There are two chapels 'Of the Fright' built on it, one Orthodox and one Catholic, and the legend that Mary fainted at the time is all too possible. A howling mob determined to lynch her eldest son must have been a terrifying experience.

What did Jesus do? What did he say when he was caught up in mob unreason and blind prejudice? If only Luke had been up on that hill at Nazareth perhaps we should have had an equally stirring tale told in his Gospel. But the only person who knew was Jesus himself, and unlike John Wesley, he didn't keep a Journal, and never told. Luke

9

must have picked the story up later from Mary or other members of Jesus' family, but they were probably not close enough in the shouting crowd to know what went on, and the amazing details are lost. But there's no doubt that 'He passed through the midst of them' covers a tale of sheer heroics.

Courage is not pretending that danger doesn't exist, but fear that has said its prayers, and in Jesus' case we see this quality in other situations too. To go into a remote graveyard to talk to a naked and uncontrollable maniac takes some guts as well, but we shall look at that story later. All in all, we have several indications that in moments of crisis he had a physical courage and 'presence' that must have been most impressive, and could still be in command of a situation when everything seemed against him.

This strength of character went with strong opinions, vehemently expressed. His criticisms of the leaders of the Jewish religion of the day were sheer vitriol. Matthew puts together a complete chapter of invective, in which one of the mildest is to call the Teachers of the Law and Pharisees 'white-washed tombs', yet even this has a hidden sting.

The Kidron Valley was a favourite place for graveyards, and still is, and in that rocky and sparse soil graves were not dug far into the ground if at all, but were either caves or stone box tombs. Jewish law said that to even touch a grave rendered a Jew unclean, so the practice was to white-wash them so that the pilgrims going to the Temple could see them clearly, avoid them, and remain ritually pure for the festivals. An almost attractive outside therefore masked the ugliness of death. In addition, it was Jewish law that it was wrong to tamper with, or move a grave for any reason whatsoever. That ground was forever unclean, and no further use could be made of that land – it was permanently 'out of commission'.

That this is still the case can be seen in Jerusalem today. The Arabs when they had control of part of the Holy City began to build a new dual-carriageway road to relieve congestion on the way across the Kidron Valley. They built from both ends over the Jewish graveyard. When the Israelis captured that part of the city, they stopped the road in its tracks. No more graves were to be disturbed, and the result is that in the middle of a good dual-carriageway to the city, there is to this day a bit that remains the old cramped road it always was, and as long as the Jews control the area, it will forever be the same.

So for Jesus to call them 'white-washed tombs' was the ultimate in insults. Not only were they a pretty outside disguising a rotten interior, but more seriously, they were also permanently rendering void, sterile, polluted and useless, the whole area of Jewish religious life. One can hardly think of a greater condemnation! No wonder the religious establishment of the day were willing to bend every rule to get rid of him.

And yet, together with this sheer strength, went a humanity that touched everyone who saw it or who has read about it since. He worked so hard sometimes that his disciples pleaded with him to rest. Yet, once when he let his disciples row him across the lake, he 'nodded off' when he should have been steering. He had times when his feet hurt – 'being wearied with the journey, he sat down by the well'. He wept sympathetically together with those who were in sorrow. He looked at Jerusalem, that Holy City whose every inch of dust is soaked with the blood of innocent and guilty, and wept over it – wept in sorrow, and wept in frustration and near-despair. And the scene on his last night in the Garden of Gethsemane is one in which we see a Jesus, strongly determined as ever, yet terrified at the same time – it is dark in Gethsemane, very dark, even today. The brighter the moonlight, the deeper the pools of shadow from the olive trees. How easy it would have been for him to slip away. But frightened as he was, he didn't; that's courage and humanity of the highest measure mixed and mingled together.

He was an eloquent public speaker. No crowd would walk for miles to hear someone unless he could make their hearts sing and their minds buzz, yet they followed every rumour that Jesus was in this area, or that. They would be so captivated, and the time would pass so quickly that they wouldn't even realize that it was getting late and that they were hungry. Anyone who goes to church regularly knows that it doesn't matter at all how long a sermon is, it is how long it seems that counts. Some preachers can make fifty minutes seem like ten, and with others after ten minutes you don't look at your watch but a calendar! Jesus was clearly the kind of speaker that 'one could listen to all day, even if they never said a thing'.

One wonders, incidentally, how many times Jesus preached the same sermons and used the same parables. In the days before radio, television and newspapers, the only way to proclaim a message widely was to tell the same thing to as many different crowds as possible. Looking at the slightly varying ways in which the four Gospels retell some of Jesus' teaching, there's no need to assume automatically that there's a fault in someone's memory, or slovenly copying of an ancient manuscript. It is quite possible in some instances at least, that the varying accounts are true records of the same sermon preached on several occasions. It is even possible, and quite natural, that his sermons improved in the repeating. It was said of that great preacher of the eighteenth century, George Whitfield, that his sermons were at their peak when he preached them for the fortieth time – after that they went downhill!

We need not imagine either that Jesus was some penniless

ascetic. Luke says that there were many women who 'ministered to him of their substance'. He had 'sponsors' like most other travelling teachers of the day, people who not only contributed to save him having to do jobbing carpenting to pay his way, but also were, no doubt, glad to provide lodging for the team when they were in the area. His tunic 'which had no seam, woven throughout in one piece from the top' was not the kind of coat for a penniless itinerant preacher. Perhaps it was a gift from one of his sponsor friends, or perhaps there is truth in the legend that it was a last present from Mary, his mother, before he went out on his preaching mission. It was in any case a gift that hid an inner meaning, for that kind of tunic was just the sort the High Priest wore.

He was also good company. Hosts seem to have delighted in inviting him to join in their parties and meals. People criticized him for being a 'glutton and a drunkard' but bearing in mind where the comment came from, we can regard that as an unjust criticism of someone who enjoyed his meals and liked the company of his fellow men.

Jesus was himself, and any label we want to stick on him peels off and falls away very quickly. People of many groups have tried to pin their badges on him and include him in their ranks. He was not a pacifist, an egalitarian, a revolutionary, a socialist, or even a 'do-gooder', although he did many things that make him look like it. We cannot tame him and stick any party label on him, and we are untrue to him if we try. He just won't fit into our modern plastic mouldings. Jesus the Man was a 'one-off'.

The New Testament translator whose modern version most loosened the straight-jacket of the traditional Bible translations of the past is Canon J.B. Phillips. In a summary of his conclusions he wrote:

The figure who emerged is quite unlike the Jesus of conventional piety, and even more unlike that imagined hero whom members of various causes claim as their champion. What we are so often confronted with today is a 'processed' Jesus. Every element that we feel is not consonant with our 'image' of him is removed, and the result is more insipid and unsatisfying than the worst of processed food.

Of course, in reality he was anything but homogenized, he was much more awkward, edgy, abrasive, and profound. Anyone who has read the Gospels recently has in all honesty to nod sagely and agree. But beware! To say this means paying a price. Oliver Wendell Holmes once said 'the world is always ready to receive talent with open arms. Very often it does not know what to do with genius.' To this we may add that the world is usually puzzled and afraid of divinity. In our search for glimpses into what Jesus was really like, we must be prepared for surprises, ready to be knocked back on our heels, willing to scrap our comfortable mental pictures of him, and be shocked into something much more realistic.

2

Joseph and Sons' Biggest Order

Jesus the lad

What happened when Jesus was young was ironic and terrifying at the same time. The experiences of one's formative years, and in particular the atmosphere of the places where one is brought up colour our character and remain in the memory for a whole life-time. Why else do people in the later years of their lives yearn to 'go home'? Nazareth, where Jesus was brought up was bound in the nature of things to have a profound effect upon his development and thinking. In particular the disaster at Sepphoris, which as far as we can tell, took place when he was a youth, must have changed him profoundly.

Nazareth was a little out of the way town, only three or four miles south of the much larger provincial centre of Sepphoris. This fortified place was the hub of the trade, politics and general activity of the area. As it was under the rule of a Roman client-king like most of Palestine, it was also a centre of Jewish disaffection and nationalist pride. Like many such cities it was ruled by people who were hung on a dilemma which is familiar to us in the twentieth century. What is one to do when living under an oppressive and unpopular regime? Some people feel that a certain basic co-operation is called for, even if only to minimize the effects on the community. Others take a much more stern view, and will plot and scheme to overthrow the oppressor at the first opportunity. In Sepphoris the two parties vied for power, and there are records of two occasions when the militants took power over the moderates and fomented a rebellion against the Romans. On the second occasion the Jewish historian Josephus, who was working for the Romans as a general at the time said:

> About this time (about AD55) the people of Sepphoris grew insolent, and took up arms, out of a confidence they had in the strength of their walls, and because they saw me engaged in other affairs also. So they sent to Cestius Gallus, who was president of Syria, and desired that either he should come quickly to them and take the city under his protection, or send them a garrison ... When I had learned so much I took the soldiers that were with me and made an assault upon the people of Sepphoris and took the city by force. The Galileans took this opportunity, thinking they now had a proper time for showing their hatred to them, since they bore ill-will to that city also ...
>
> So they ran upon them, and set their houses on fire ... they carried off everything and omitted no kind of desolation.

This gives a flavour of the smouldering anti-Roman feeling within Sepphoris, shows the overwhelming ease with which the Romans could snuff out a provincial revolt, and also gives a glimpse into the 'country versus city' resentment.

This defeat was a re-run of a previous revolt which had taken place a generation or so earlier while Jesus was a lad, and was equally easily put down. Easily but not bloodlessly. A punitive expedition of Roman soldiers breached the proud walls, devastated the town, and crucified a large part of the population. Joseph and Mary with their growing family must have watched the marching armies pass, seen the preparations, even perhaps been visited by Romans buying or commandeering food, tools, and materials for the seige. Being such a short distance away, they must have heard the noise of battle, seen the rising smoke of burning buildings, and followed every development with horrified fascination.

Perhaps they helped refugees who were, in terror, escaping from the city, and possibly they may have even made preparations to escape themselves if the fighting spread. We don't know what political views the family held; were they hoping that the city held out, did they think the revolutionaries were getting what they deserved, or did they just hope peace would return as soon as possible? The fighting ended, as all realists knew it would, with the usual Roman systematic bloodshed. To ensure that it never happened again, the Romans crucified a large part of the population of what was a busy city. It is said that the numbers ran into many thousands.

Where did the Romans get the crosses from? That many crosses would demand a considerable quantity of wood, and even crude crosses need a certain minimum of carpentry. Did the soldiers do the work, or did they make their prisoners do it themselves? Or did they – and what a heart-breaking irony if it is true – did they call on the services of all the carpenters in the surrounding towns and villages? There is at least a possibility that one day at the end of the seige, a group of Roman soldiers stopped outside the carpenters shop in Nazareth for a worrying moment, went in, and ordered Joseph and his sons to make a very large number of crosses, and quickly. It could easily have been that the largest order that little village carpenter ever had was for the Roman Department of Defence! We can be sure that such an order, however lucrative, for the means of executing hundreds of his fellow-countrymen, is one that Joseph would much rather have done without.

Jesus as a boy and teenager must have known Sepphoris intimately. Even a fairly self-contained place like Nazareth had needs which could not be supplied locally. So, for the complicated part or the unusual material, it must have been a regular thing for the older children to have been sent over the hill to the nearest big city to buy it. As the eldest son, the young Jesus must have travelled that journey many times. Joseph would have been busy at his work, Mary preoccupied with the housework and the small children, it must have been a great day for the family when Jesus was old enough and responsible enough to be trusted to do important errands like that by himself. He must have become familiar with the markets and the shops, the roads and the civic buildings. As the visiting 'country boy', he would have been nervous at first, but gradually gaining in confidence as he found his way around, and as his brothers grew up he would have taken them with him and introduced them to the sights and sounds of the 'big city'.

So to hear and see the city he knew well being destroyed, to know that many of the trades-people he had dealt with were suffering an agonizing execution on crosses that were even, as we have seen, possibly made by him or his father, must have been a traumatic shock to a young man growing up. If ever any experience could have underlined the futility of revolt against the Romans it must have been that. If Jesus was to introduce a new Kingdom, it had to be 'a Kingdom not of this world'.

With hindsight we can see an almost unbearable fact, the shadow of his own personal cross has not gone away with any renunciation of violence he may have made at the time, but inexorably reaches forward over him. The simple, carefree childhood in the rustic back-water of Nazareth had come to a violent end.

By the first century Nazareth was just a small conservative town up in the hills, not really on the way to anywhere. Although it was only a day's walk to the Mediterranean Sea on one side and the Lake of Galilee on the other, and various roads led from it, no 'through traffic' ever had need to use its streets. It seems to have been neglected by everyone, it is not mentioned anywhere in the Old Testament, nor by Josephus the Jewish historian. In fact it was such an undistinguished place that John records a man called Nathanael saying that it wasn't the sort of place that anything good was likely to come from.

However, though it was off the main road, it was an excellent vantage point to see what was going on. One only had to climb the hill on which the town was set to get a magnificent view of that part of the country, and onlookers at the time could have seen the passing pilgrims going to Jerusalem, trading caravans from Egypt and Midian, Roman legions and princes' retinues. In fact the view reeked with history, it was possible to see Gilboa where the freedom fighter Gideon fought, and King Saul died; the three magnificent snow-covered peaks of Mount Hermon which according to the Psalms 'sing for joy'. The river Kishon lay in the valley, the most fought over place in the world, on the shores of which the grim Elijah slew the prophets of Baal, and beside it countless armies had marched and counter-marched to victory or death. Jesus' religious education was not set in places far away, but on his doorstep, in the background of the places he could see, and in the fields where he could walk.

The 'Virgin's Spring' is the only water supply in Nazareth, now as it was then, and even with stored rainwater cisterns, it must have limited the size of the population able to live there. As one climbs down into the old well chamber today, one can easily imagine the young mother Mary filling her water pot there several times a day, accompanied by the toddler Jesus, holding on to her skirts. One can also justifiably think of teenagers gathering there in an evening after the day's work was done, to chat and giggle and philsophize, much as they do today outside fish and chip shops, and in town centres.

The religious training Jesus had would have been based on two places, the home and the Synagogue school. The genius of Jewish religious practice has always been the strong emphasis on family devotions. The stories he would first have heard would have been about the saints and heroes of his own nation, associated with many of the sites he could actually see from the hill behind the town. Then, as the years passed, punctuated by the Jewish festivities in the home, he would gradually see their significance, and realize why they were so valued.

The Feast of Hanukkah, held in mid-winter, commemorated the triumph of the Maccabees, and their restoration of true religion. Day by day candles were lit, an additional one on every day, until the festival day. In early spring the Festival of Purim, the Feast of the deliverance of the Jews by Esther, was celebrated with great merriment and exchanging of presents. Then came the great solemnity of Passover. Most people went to Jerusalem for it, but even if they did, there was still the careful torchlight search in every nook and cranny of the house to get rid of the least crumb of leaven. Later came harvest, rich with ceremony and significance. After that came the Feast of New Year, with sober thoughts of the stewardship of time and responsibility. This was followed by the fast of the Day of Atonement, with its discipline and tremendous solemnity, which led to the delightful Feast of Tabernacles, when one lived in a tent in the garden and thought of things becoming new.

Each of these events, in which the growing children

took an active part, was redolent of past history, and ringing with the echoes of godly principles. A child could not be brought up in a household like that without absorbing a great grounding of faith in God. Not only was Jesus picking up all this, incidentally, as it were, but he would have been expected to learn formally as well. As soon as he was able to take it in he would have been taught a little summary of faith and his birthday text. That done, he then went on to learn his first Psalms. 'When Israel came out of Egypt' and 'I will lift up mine eyes to the hills', were two of the ones Jewish children had to learn first. Such was the kind of home background that Jesus had.

When he was six, Jesus went to school. The education system of the day was intensive and carefully co-ordinated. One of the rules was that teachers should have exactly the same conditions as the pupils, so they usually all sat in circles on the ground. As soon as a boy was old enough he was started on the Book of Leviticus, and then taken through the first four books of the Bible. After that, he was then guided through the Prophetic Books of the Old Testament and the Ethical ones. From the age of ten, he graduated to the wearisome study of the commentaries on the books, and when he reached fifteen he started on higher theological discussions. We can make the fair assumption that in an orthodox out-of-the-way place like Nazareth, the Bible study would have been done methodically and traditionally, with few modern touches. The wide knowledge which Jesus clearly had of the Jewish scriptures was based on years of solid study during this period. But far from squeezing him into a mould, he thought his own thoughts, reached his own conclusions, and followed his own inspiration with scandalous consequences, as we shall see later.

There were three ceremonies which Jesus would have

gone through, in common with all male children. When he was eight days old he would have been circumcised, and at this time his name of Jesus (meaning 'The Lord is Salvation') was given to him. One complication was that in the case of a first-born, which Jesus was, there was associated with it a second ceremony, the rite of redemption. According to the Old Testament every first-born male belonged to God, and had to be 'redeemed' after the first month with a sizeable payment of five shekels. It is interesting that Luke, who alone tells us anything about the childhood of Jesus doesn't mention the 'redemption of Jesus'. Is it because, though Mary told him about it, as a Gentile he didn't realize its significance? Or did it happen that Mary and Joseph didn't 'buy Jesus back', but presented him permanently as God's servant?

A third ritual concerned Mary, for every woman was regarded as ceremonially unclean for forty days after the birth, and was not allowed to take part in public worship. She had to take a lamb, and turtle dove, or young pigeon to the Temple to be sacrificed. Now this could be expensive! So for poor people allowances were made, and instead of the lamb, they could substitute a second dove or pigeon. Though Joseph and Mary travelled the three days journey to Jerusalem to do it, the ordinary nature of the family is underlined when we notice that it was this 'offering of the poor' that Mary made for her purification.

The next ceremony occurred when Jesus was twelve years old, the equivalent of confirmation. At that age a boy was expected to accept for himself the religious responsibilities and duties which had up to then been borne on his behalf by his parents. For this, the whole family, and others too, travelled to Jerusalem, and what happened then gave rise to the only story about Jesus' childhood to be recorded.

Every year his parents used to go to Jerusalem for the feast of the Passover. When he was twelve years of age, when they went up according to the custom of the feast, and when they had completed the days of the feast, when they returned home the child Jesus stayed on in Jerusalem. His parents were not aware of this. They thought he was in the caravan and when they had gone a day's journey they looked for him among their kinsfolk and acquaintances. When they did not find him they turned back to Jerusalem, looking for him all the time. After three days they found him in the temple precincts, sitting in the middle of the Rabbis, listening to them and asking them questions. All who were listening were astonished at his understanding and at his answers.

When they saw him they were amazed. His mother said to him, 'child, why did you do this to us? Look here, your father and I have been looking for you and we have been very worried.' He said to them, 'Why were you looking for me? Did you not know that I was bound to be in my Father's house?' They did not understand the meaning of what he said to them. So he came home with them and went to Nazareth and he was obedient to them. His mother kept all these things in her heart. And Jesus grew wise and grew bigger and increased in favour with God and man.

In this story one can almost hear Mary talking. As we shall discover later in our investigation, Luke's Gospel seems to breathe first-hand accounts, particularly about the events early in Jesus' life. As a careful and punctilious author he seems to have gone to great trouble to get to the root of what actually happened. Whether he went to Nazareth himself, or whether he met Mary somewhere else we do not know, but he certainly managed to obtain stories of what went on there, stories that ring true.

23

Any parent knows the heart-stopping nightmare of losing a young child. Children are so easily distracted, they live for the moment and can so easily wander off and get lost in crowded streets. All parents would also know the frantic searching, the fears of the worst which are pushed to the back of one's mind, the utter relief when the child is found in the last place one expects to find him, and the way that the joy is expressed in scolding and displeasure. Experiences like that make a scar on any mother's or father's memory, and are never forgotten. How utterly natural it is that when Luke was asking Mary to tell him stories of the childhood of Jesus, the first to occur to her was this traumatic time when they lost him for three days and nights in the crowds of the big city.

It all happened so easily too. The usual method of travel was that the women and children would set off early on the first day as they walked more slowly. Later the men, moving faster, would set off, and meet up with them at the first overnight stop. The journey on which this accident occurred was when Jesus was at the twelve year old change from childhood to manhood. How natural it was then, when Mary set off home with the younger children, for her to assume that the young Jesus, now twelve, would achieve his long ambition of travelling with the grown-up men. It was also natural that Joseph, not seeing Jesus anywhere, would have assumed that he had departed earlier with the women and other children, as he normally did. One can imagine the conversation between them when they met that night and the terrible truth dawned. 'I thought he was with you.' 'And I assumed, naturally, that he was with you.' 'Then where is he?' One can then assume the arrangements and plans that were made, should Joseph go back by himself, leaving Mary to take the other children home? But she would be too worried to do that, and two searchers are better than one.

Obviously someone else would have to care for the young ones while they both went back to look.

But that was the only problem we had with him, one can almost hear Mary say in the words Luke records. 'He wasn't any trouble really, he was a good lad, sensible, and everybody liked him.' How else can one express in a mother's words, 'He increased in favour with God and man.'

As he grew he was joined by a growing family. We know from Mark that there were at least seven children in the family; Jesus had four brothers and at least two sisters: 'Is this not the carpenter, the son of Mary, and brother of James, Joses, Judas, and Simon? and are not his sisters here with us?'

Eldest sons tend to have responsibility thrown upon them early, and cannot express the carefree attitudes of the younger children. Though we have no stories about it that are authentic, we can assume that often Jesus was in the position of having to settle squabbles and even fights between his younger brothers and sisters. It is poignant that one of them should have the same name, Simon, as his right-hand man through his ministry, and another, Judas, the name of the man who betrayed that ministry to a bloody end. And as the children grew up, became adult, married and had children of their own, it is easy to see him congratulating brides and grooms, feeling the tight grips of little babies' fingers, and generally spoiling his nephews and nieces. As a carpenter it requires no stretch of the imagination to picture him making the toys that the children of those days played with, rattles, pull-along animals, dolls and dolls houses. With his deep interest in religion, one can also justifiably guess that he was well involved in the spiritual training of these children, and the target of many difficult childish questions. 'I don't know the answer to that one, go and ask your uncle Jesus.'

It is also easy to imagine the good-natured match-making that must have gone on between his brothers and sisters-in-law. How often people must have said 'If only he'd find a nice Jewish girl and settle down – why didn't he marry that nice Esther who was so sweet on him, they would have made a lovely couple.' To his family the unmarried Jesus must have seemed somehow different, apart. His aims were totally elsewhere.

When Joseph died we do not know, he is not directly mentioned after the Jerusalem episode. From this it is assumed that he was much older than Mary and died soon after, leaving Jesus to take over as head of the family and bread-winner. If so, it would seem that Jesus stayed working as a jobbing builder, working not only in wood, but also stone, and mud-brick, until he was about 30, and his brothers were able to take over the running of the family business, so freeing him to achieve what he felt called by God to do.

This sense of 'call' clearly consumed him. A new Kingdom of God! But where did he fit into it? How was it to be achieved? Some people think that Jesus knew everything from the beginning, and he had no need of spiritual development. But this destroys his humanity, and his oneness with us. As one reads the New Testament, one can see how he felt his call confirmed at the River Jordan, how he thrashed out his methods on the Mount of Temptation, how he realized that the secret was not in self-assertion, but in self-giving, and how he agonized when he discovered the cost of it.

Of one thing he was certain, the trauma of Sepphoris which had etched into his soul in his younger days had convinced him that no new regime worth having could be achieved by blood, fire and sword. It had to be new, drastic, and revolutionary, yet how could it ever justify the nightmare sights which created cities full of widows and orphans. The Kingdom of God could not be propped up by a forest of wooden crosses dripping with blood. And yet . . .?

3

A Man of his Time

Jesus the Jew

The Greek goddess Aphrodite, whom the Romans called Venus, was the goddess of love, and according to Greek mythology emerged from the sea fully formed and ready for action on the beaches of Cyprus, (or perhaps it was the island of Cythera). She had no background, no past history, no culture from which she sprang – no roots; it was the perfect neutral insertion of the divine into human life.

This can't be said about Jesus. Born approximately 4 BC in a little village up in the Judean hills, brought up in an unknown and poor Jewish family and influenced by the political and religious ideas of his community – there was nothing neutral about him. He comes to us in the Gospels not as a sterile, antiseptic saviour, but one with dust on his hands and mud on his feet – smelling of the earthy political antagonisms and clashing religious interests of the time. Jesus was a Jew, a Jew from Galilee, and must have worked, played, looked and sounded like one. The influence of God upon him was not divorced from the world in which he was brought up, but coloured by it, and filtered through it. It is no service to the timeless and placeless Christ of Faith, to weaken the human Jesus who was firmly grown at a particular time and in a specific location. We can see more about him and his significance if we look at the influences upon him as he grew. How far did he 'go along' with the religious ideas of his age, and how far did he reject and supersede them?

A few months ago a Jewish Rabbi, a long-standing friend, startled me by saying 'Well, of course, Jesus was a Pharisee.'

The more I thought about it the more I came to the conclusion that he might well be at least partially right. Jesus was more like a Pharisee, a renegade and reforming one, perhaps, but more like a Pharisee than any other religious type in Palestine at that time. But what about those terrible condemnations and curses against the Pharisees which we read in the Gospels? 'Isaiah was right when he prophesied about you hypocrites ... You have let go of the commands of God and are holding on to the traditions of men.' His favourite words for them were 'A brood of vipers', and 'hypocrites'. Jesus condemned their legalism, the formality of their religious practices, and their insufferable self-righteousness. And yet he spent a great deal of time arguing with them, far more than with the other groups. Nicodemus, who became a secret follower of Jesus, was a Pharisee, as was the Apostle Paul. Why was he so close to the people he attacked so much? When one thinks about it, it is ordinary human nature that the closest people come in for the greatest criticism. Those with whom we don't come into contact, or whose ideas are foreign to us seem largely to escape. Perhaps Jesus had come under their influence in his formative years, and gradually came to reject them. They were, after all, the largest religious movement in the country, comprised mostly of ordinary laymen, not priests.

The name Pharisees meant 'The Separated Ones', and they set themselves the onerous task of trying to keep the Jewish Law in every detail. They were not a conservative reactionary group, but tried instead to apply the Jewish Law to every aspect of life as it developed. The essential heart of the Law 'Love God and love your neighbour' was protected in their minds by a fence of minor regulations which would protect them against coming within reach of breaking the Law of God. For instance the commandment not to work on the Sabbath Day was elaborated into a forest of 'don'ts'. Amongst them were rules about not lighting fires in their houses, not carrying any load, and not walking more than one kilometre from their homes. Many Pharisees were sincere and dedicated people, and were held in high esteem by ordinary people, but they tended to regard themselves as a spiritual elite, and looked down on Jews who were not so punctilious, whom they called 'sinners'.

They were a lay movement and the largest of the Jewish sects, so were everywhere and could have been a strong influence in the Nazareth Synagogue where Jesus was brought up. As strict and dedicated religious people, with a sprinkling of very holy and wise men, their very serious pursuit of Godliness would by itself have had an attraction for most idealistic young men, maybe Jesus among them. There is no evidence for or against, but it is quite possible that as the young Jesus developed he might have been at first strongly attracted by the Pharisees, for complete dedication has a magnetic attraction. But when he fully understood their legalistic methods he could have been just as strongly repelled.

Another tradition could have influenced Jesus – the Galilean history of charismatic religious leaders. There seems to have been something in the Galilean culture and temperament which spawned and nurtured a series of religious leaders who claimed to have supernatural abilities derived from their contact with God.

The one best known to us, and presumably well known

to Jesus, was a renowned and saintly man called 'Honi the circle drawer' after his exploits as a rain-maker. He lived in the first century BC and was stoned to death by a mob in Jerusalem. Another who lived slightly later than Jesus and came from a city just ten miles north of Nazareth was Hanina Ben Dosa. He was not only a very godly man but a man who could perform miraculous healings, in person and at a distance. Interestingly, although he was consulted by the rich and famous, even by the renowned teacher Gamaliel, he was also regarded with some suspicion and resentment by the Pharisees.

When one considers the way that Jesus healed the sick, exorcised demons and seemed to have powers over natural events to the point of walking on water and stilling a storm, we can see that Galilee could be the natural home for these things. In such a soil this side of Jesus's ministry could grow, where such events, though always surprising, would not be regarded as incredible.

Travelling south down the sweltering hot valley to the Dead Sea from Jericho, on the right there is a plateau beside a deep watercourse which cuts down the high limestone cliffs and on it lies the monastic settlement of Qumran. It is now world-famous because when the people who lived there were attacked by the Roman army in 63 AD, they buried their sacred books in the surrounding caves. The first manuscripts were found by a wandering Arab goatherd called Mohammed the Wolf in 1947; together they are known as the Dead Sea Scrolls. These scrolls, preserved by the dry heat, are a thousand years earlier than any other Old Testament manuscripts, but equally importantly they have given us details of a religious movement of Jesus' time about which we knew very little, the Essenes. This could be another group which had an influence on Jesus.

The Essenes started about 150 BC when a group of

priests, led by a man called 'The Teacher of Righteousness' gathered round him a 'Council of Twelve' and broke away from the Temple in Jerusalem. They were even stricter than the Pharisees whom they thought of as slapdash 'givers of easy interpretations'. Rejecting the new Greek calendar, they made almost a fetish of personal and ritual cleanliness, (hence the site near a stream, and an enormous and complicated water system), thought the world was coming to an end soon, and retired to the wilderness to prepare for it. On the Sabbath they joined together for a meal of bread and wine, and as a foretaste of heaven, celebrated on festival days with a 'Love Banquet' Though small and exclusive in number, their spiritual single-mindedness and obvious dedication had its attraction for many people, and they sent out members of their group to preach and baptize in water, a reflection of their own initiation rites at Qumran.

Obviously Jesus wasn't an Essene; he wasn't strict enough, and didn't worry about ritual cleanliness; but there are enough similarities between what they did and believed, and how his subsequent ministry worked out, to make it probable that he knew about them. And if Jesus wasn't an Essene, his cousin John almost certainly was. The familiar picture of a desert preacher, called 'The Baptizer', accompanied by a crowd of disciples, who would not eat bread or drink wine, dressed in homespun camel hair, and preaching a fire and brimstone message of the end of the world, fits into the Essene pattern like a glove. By the accounts in the Gospels and Jewish history John was successful too; he drew large crowds, and baptized many converts in the river Jordan.

There was clearly a good mutual relationship between Jesus and John, one that may have been of many years standing. Each had a high opinion of the other. John saw Jesus as someone who was in a different league from himself, 'whose sandals I am not fit to carry' and Jesus regarded John as more than a prophet, 'the greatest man who ever lived'. A relationship like that doesn't come about by hearsay.

What was possibly the crucial turning point of Jesus' life took place in the company of John – the time when Jesus went to John to be baptized in Jordan. It's an intriguing event, whose meaning has puzzled theologians ever since it happened. Why did Jesus need to be baptized at all? Perhaps the simplest solution is to see it as Jesus' 'Call to the Ministry'. Over many years Jesus had grown in his understanding and perception of God, possibly after profound conversations with John the Baptist. One can easily imagine subjects where they would both agree, and others where they would not. Jesus did not feel that the Essene way was right for him, yet retained a tremendous respect for John as a godly man.

At this point in his life he felt the hand of God upon him to leave the family and the business and do what he felt God was impelling him to do. To mark this turning point he offered himself to be baptized by his friend and relation John, and underwent what turned out to be a tremendous spiritual experience, which like all such experiences, can only be described in picturesque figurative language. The Essene influence on Jesus must have been profound.

There were other religious groups in the country which had less effect on him. The 'Hasidim' (the Pious Ones) were not an organized sect, but a movement of people who defended Jewish culture against the inroads of Greek and Roman ideas. Some dedicated themselves to armed struggle, others were pacifists, and many joined the Pharisees or the Essenes.

Another movement was the Zealots, who were strict nationalists. They kept alive the spirit of the great Jewish revolutionary leader Judas Maccabaeus, refused to pay taxes to the Romans, and plotted and prepared for armed revolt. Interestingly, though Jesus clearly rejected a military way of bringing in the Kingdom of God, he included among his twelve disciples one of them, 'Simon, who was called The Zealot'. Perhaps he was or had been a Zealot, or maybe 'who was called' is a clue that it may have been a nickname, a joking description of a man who was always complaining about the Romans, or conversely was so meek and mild that he never did!

One final main group was the Sadducees. They were a small but influential group of upper-class Jewish families who supported the Roman rulers whose interests were more political than religious. As far as we can tell (and we don't know much about them) they rejected the rules and regulations of the Pharisees, and stuck to an ancient interpretation of the Old Testament, which is why they denied the resurrection of the dead. According to what evidence we have Jesus didn't come up against them until his final trials.

Taking them all together, we can see that Jesus did not grow up in a sterile moral test-tube, but his spiritual development took place amid the claims and counter-claims of competing religious groups. His unique and individual message was rooted in the troubled situation of his own time. It was not a sudden light in a dark room, but one lamp among many, the one that kept burning when the rest went out. At the time it was one shout in an uproar, the one that could still be heard when the others fell silent.

The climate and geography of any country seems to affect the temperament of the people who live there. There's every reason to think that the Galilee area where Jesus lived was a profound influence upon him too. As the great Lake of Galilee/Dead Sea rift indicates, it is earthquake country, and once off the hills it is a lush and fertile semi-tropical land. He obviously enjoyed living there and knew enough about the countryside and lakeside to be able to use many parallels and analogies in his sermons. His ideal of ultimate beauty was the flowering meadows – the lilies of the field – and the depth of wickedness was deliberately to sow weeds in someone's cornfield, even if that field belonged to one's enemy.

The cities and their teeming life, full of illustrations for modern preachers, had very little appeal to him, for what he knew about the was countryside. Take, for example, his parable about the seed corn, some of which would not grow among thorns. Why didn't it? After all, thorns and thistles grow quite happily in England surrounded by ears of wheat. But if one looks closely at the thorns and thistles in Palestine one can see that as the lower leaves dry and drop, they make a small wigwam of dead leaves several inches thick at the foot of the plant. Any scattered seeds sown there would not reach the soil in order to sprout, and even if they did would get no light and be smothered. This is a phenomenon Jesus must have noticed.

Another example of Jesus being country-wise is his knowledge of the Sea of Galilee. There are, and were, some seventeen kinds of fish in the lake. One of the smallest is a sardine or sprat, which is still trawled at night, and is now canned at a Kibbutz on the shore and exported to one of Britain's best known chain stores. At the time it was salted and dried in order to preserve it, and these were probably the 'two small fishes' which the little boy had at the Feeding of the Five Thousand.

The main reason why salt was so important at that time was not so much to flavour food as to preserve it. The Dead Sea was a rich source of salt, and the lakeside village of Magdala in Galilee, where Mary Magdalene came from, was the main fish preserving centre of the Lake. As the Dead Sea salt contained a large proportion of phosphates and other chemicals, it was also used as fertiliser.

Another fish in Galilee, the Musht, is larger, about ten inches long. An ugly and bony fish, it is delicious when cooked. It has an unusual way of protecting its young, for it allows them to excape predators by swimming back into the parent's large mouth. This is an activity which the parent fish apparently finds quite tiresome after the early days, so to prevent an undignified rush by youngsters who are big enough to look after themselves the parent Musht picks up a stone from the bottom of the lake, of the right size to fill up its mouth, preventing anything else from getting in. This adds new light to Jesus' conversation with Peter about paying taxes: 'Go the lake and throw out your line. Take the first fish you catch; open its mouth and you will find a four drachma (shekel) coin. Take it and give it to them for my tax and yours.' The miracle here, told for whatever reason, is not that the coin should be found in the fish, for that particular coin is the exact size that the fish would be looking for to fill its mouth. The coin was almost certainly a Shekel of Tyre, which was not only struck over a long period, and circulating freely in that area, but was actually specified in Jewish Law, with its half-shekel, to be used in paying the tribute. It was silver, with a portrait on one side and an eagle on the other, and was one inch in diameter. It is entirely natural that a fish, looking for the right sized stone on the bottom of the lake, should have its attention drawn to this a coin which is brighter and smoother than a stone, and pick it up instead. The miracle is that Jesus knew that it had done it. For this reason the Musht is now known as 'St Peter's Fish'.

A third kind of fish in the Lake of Galilee is the sort the little Mushts were hiding from, the formidable snapper-up of smaller fish, the cat-fish, or Barbut. It is larger, has cartilage instead of a backbone, does not have scales or fins, squeaks when out of water and can live out of its natural element for up to four days. As it does not have bones, and has snake-like characteristics, it is forbidden in the Book of Leviticus to all Jews as unclean food. In common language it was called a serpent. This makes clear what Jesus meant when he said: 'Which of you if your son asks . . . for a fish will give him a serpent?' In other words, 'if your son asks for a Musht, which is religiously kosher, would you give him a Barbut, which is not? Then neither does your heavenly Father give you what will make you unclean.' Here we see not only Jesus' familiarity with the countryside around him, but also his acceptance of some, at least, of the Jewish dietary laws, either for himself, or in deference to his hearers.

A fascinating insight into one of Jesus' local loyalties occurs in the place that is never mentioned. Like the Sherlock Holmes' dog that didn't bark in the night, what is remarkable is the place that Jesus never went to, as far as we know, and never gets a reference in any of the Gospels. Jesus in fact rarely mentions any of the larger places of Palestine, but this one was a 'must'.

If anyone were to compile a gazetteer of Galilee, then and now, however short it was, one place had to be top of the list. Set on the side of the Sea of Galilee it was the famous spa centre of the country, hot sulphurous water came bubbling out of the hillside and poured into the lake, and it was noted in those days for its healing waters. It was only six miles round the shore from Jesus' headquarters at Capernaum yet it never gets even a passing mention. A proud, newly-built spa town built on the shore – ignored! Why? The reason is simple. The town dated back to Solomon, but was rebuilt by Herod Antipas in AD 17 and called Tiberias as flattery to the reigning Roman Emperor. Even the lake was renamed The Sea of Tiberias.

Just south of the town by the hot springs was a crag upon which Herod Antipas had built a castle for the devious plottings and artificial pleasures of his oriental court. The ordinary Galilee people, who before this had revelled in the delights of the area, distrusted Herod, despised his new town, and avoided both like the plague. Perhaps it was typical Galilean chauvinism, but they never visited it and never talked about it unless they had to. And by all accounts Jesus took the same attitude, for he called Herod Antipas, the man who had executed John the Baptist, 'that fox', which had a ruder connotation then than it has to us today. The result is that the town of Tiberias, the most prestigious place on the lake, is never mentioned in the Gospels, and as far as we know, Jesus never went there.

Which brings us to the fact that Jesus was a Galilean himself. There are various accounts of what Galileans were like as a people, some from those who were prejudiced against them, mainly the religious authorities in the south, some from politicians who regarded them all as 'trouble', and there's Josephus, the Jewish historian, from whom we get a more even-handed account. There was a clear-cut regional divide between north and south Palestine, a difference in tradition, culture, temperament and speech.

To the Rabbis in the south the northerner was a figure of fun or an ignoramus, perhaps both. One of the classic Jerusalem jokes was based on the fact that the Galilean did not speak Aramaic properly. The story revolved round the word 'hamar' which if pronounced in slightly different ways meant either a donkey, wine, wool or a lamb, and the Jerusalem shop-keeper couldn't make out which the Galilean wanted. The Galilean speech was softer and the guttural sounds either sounded very like each other, or disappeared altogether. Put simply, the Galileans dropped their 'aitches', and this made them difficult for southerners to understand. Some places in the north were so notorious for it that people from them were forbidden when visiting the south from reading the scriptures in public. That Jesus was the same is clear in the account of his friends, Mary, Martha and Lazarus. The name Lazarus is the 'incorrect' Galilean dialect version of Eleazar. In a later chapter we shall look at the Aramaic words Jesus used, which were the Galilean dialect of the language, not the 'correct' Jerusalem version.

Not only this but Galileans had the reputation for being very slap-dash and unorthodox in their observance of religious duties, and punctilious priests in the south would require much more proof from a Galilean than anyone else that the proper rituals had been observed and the proper sacrifices made. In short, however educated or holy they might be, they were regarded as 'peasants'.

Politically they were 'bad news'. From the middle of the previous century Galilee had been the hotbed of all the revolutionary movements. It is probable that the whole Zealot movement sprang from the members of one Galilean family, but it soon spread from a family business to inflame the whole of Galilee. The 'god-father' of the family, Ezekias, was executed by Herod the Great, but the rebellious leadership was handed down from father to son, until the last of them, Eleazar, the legendary captain of Masada, perished in the final cataclysm in AD 73. The bloodiest, and most notorious leaders of the AD 66–73 war were Galileans, so it's not surprising that to the 'powers that were' in the south, they represented political trouble. To accept a Galilean as a half-educated buffoon was one thing, but together with it went a mafia-like reputation for vindictive and callous bloodshed.

As we have seen, Jesus himself was not a Zealot, and had experienced in Sepphoris the uselessness of armed rebellion. Yet when eventually he was tried in Jerusalem, he was certainly charged, prosecuted and sentenced as one. To the eyes of a member of the Jerusalem establishment, Jew, Greek or Roman, any Galilean with a popular following, if not a rebel then, would soon become one. Josephus in his history infers that Jesus was crucified because he won over many Jews. Paradoxically, had Jesus not been successful in his preaching he would have been in no danger. Had he not spoken with a Galilean accent, and been the centre of a group of Galileans, he might have been tolerated – at least by the civil power. But he was condemned precisely because he was so Galilean, so rooted in his culture, so representative of a rebellious people.

'Guilt by Association' is the modern name for it. It is an ironic quirk of history which points to a theological truth that he died, not because he was personally guilty, but because he rooted himself among a guilty people.

4

The Shameful Stones

His headquarters

In an empty field – overgrown and derelict – by the side of
the Lake of Galilee, there is an area which is being
excavated by archaeologists. Like all such sites, it is a
confusing jumble of trenches, pits, and what look like
random heaps of stones. But at one end of the field there is
a re-erected building, or at least enough of it to show what
it was. It was discovered between 1905 and 1926 and has
proved to be the ruins of a very old Jewish synagogue, and
built into its walls were things that were surprising,
shocking and shameful. For they are stones carved with
Roman regimental badges and medals. To patriotic Jews
they would have been at the time a disgrace – more than
that, an outrage! How did they get there? Who put them
there, and why?

The site we are looking at is what remains of Capernaum,
the headquarters of Jesus – as far as he had one – during his
teaching ministry, and at the time one of the fishing and
market centres of Galilee. The ruins of this synagogue date
from the AD 300s, but it was built over the black basalt
foundations of a smaller previous synagogue on the site.
However, even if what we can see is 300 years later than
the time of Jesus, carved stones of this elaborate kind
would quite likely have been rescued from a falling-down

old building and re-erected in the new one. We can with some confidence assume that this synagogue, or its predecessor on the site, from which these stones were rescued, was the place where he worshipped and taught.

So where did these stones come from? What is Jesus' connection with them? It is a fascinating story full of clues and small bits of surprising evidence, for it's possible to follow the trail like a detective sniffing out a mystery.

When Jesus was hounded out of his home town of Nazareth, he had to decide where to make his next base. Even a wandering preacher has to have a home somewhere! When I last had a discussion with the Income Tax authorities about my permanent address, they defined my 'home' as where I kept my old clothes. When Jesus was rejected by the old fashioned and orthodox religious people of Nazareth, he had to decide where he would, from then on, keep his old clothes.

Would he opt for the centre of religious life, the gritty, tumultuous, dangerous city of Jerusalem? He knew it well, had visited it three times a year for the 'Pilgrim Festivals' – Passover, Pentecost, and Tabernacles – as all good Jews did, knew his way around it, and had friends in the city, especially in the city's Galilean suburb of Bethany. Lazarus, and his sisters Mary and Martha would be only too pleased to find him house-room. Would he choose to start afresh where he wasn't known, and go west to the civilized Greek cities of the coast, Tyre, Sidon, or Caesarea? Or the ten Greek towns just across the lake, known collectively as the Decapolis? They were very close, and near to home.

No. He chose none of these, but elected instead to go north to Capernaum. Why? One reason is immediately obvious. Of all the little villages and towns surrounding the lake – and there were many more than there are now – Capernaum was the hub. To this bustling town were brought all the fish that were for sale on the lake, dried or fresh. Fishing boats continually unloaded their catches, and cargo boats from across the lake brought cloth, pottery and all the handicrafts village craftsmen could make. Farmers sent the fruit and vegetables they could so easily grow on the fertile soil, and in the warm subtropical climate. For while Nazareth, Jesus' home, was in the hills, a lofty 1300 feet above sea-level, Capernaum was a warm 682 feet below. The larger boats even brought exotic goods, silks and spices, from Damascus and further east, for the lake crossing was easier than toiling round the edge.

For anyone wanting to spread a message Capernaum was the place to be – everyone came there at one time or another. It was the centre of the local web; say something significant there, and it was all round Galilee in no time at all.

The ruins there now, and the depth of water, show that the harbour and lakeside warehouses spread over a third of a mile of shore. The town was one vast market, teeming with buyers and sellers – smooth city gents from Phoenicia on the coast, exotic traders from Damascus, suspicious Greeks from the Decapolis, and eminent ecclesiastics from Jerusalem. Along the jetties would be fishermen, shipwrights, dockers, all busy in their own trade, absorbed in making their own living. Camel trains, loaded donkeys and ox-carts loaded high with goods would cram the roads and pile up at the customs house.

For another reason why Capernaum was so busy was the fact that it was a frontier town. It was on the northern border of the territory which Herod Antipas, one of the sons of Herod the Great, held under the Romans. The Road of the Sea, the great coastal highway coming all the way from Egypt, struck inland at this point, to avoid the coastal malarial marshes, and passed through Capernaum.

It then branched, the right fork to Itrurea, the territory of another of Herod's sons, Philip, the left fork to the Greek cities of Phoenicia and back to the sea. This is why Capernaum was one of the few towns in Palestine to have a permanent Roman garrison, commanded by a centurion.

It was also why it had a customs house and a regular staff of tax officials manning the little booths on the border road. Among those customs men was Levi, to give him his Jewish name, or Matthew, to give him his Greek name. For most people, particularly those who came into regular contact with both Jewish and Greek culture, had two names. Matthew was Customs and Excise, not Inland Revenue.

It was Matthew who innocently caused one of the biggest scandals during Jesus' ministry in Capernaum. Having responded to the call to leave the customs booth and 'follow me', it was only natural that Matthew should decide to throw a final party for his work-mates. It is also natural that he should invite the teacher whom he was now going to follow to attend, and that he should want to introduce him to his erstwhile colleagues. This was just not done in Jewish circles. Even the pagan writer Lucian linked tax-gatherers with 'adulterers, flatterers and syco-phants', and the attitude of the Jews towards people collecting taxes for the Romans was even less compli-mentary! Any Jew who had any dealings with a Gentile was automatically ceremonially unclean, and customs men to whom these contacts were an essential part of their job could not hope to be acceptable in religious circles. So for this newly arrived Rabbi to go to a tax-gatherers house, meet a crowd of them and actually eat with them was too much!

This, then, was the general situation in Capernaum – a busy, provincial market town, which Jesus chose as the headquarters of his ministry.

At the heart of the town was, of course, the Synagogue. The present ruins are of an imposing stone building, complete with water canal for ritual washings, a stairway, prayer hall, gallery for the women, and an outside court-yard. Its predecessor, which presumably was the one in which Jesus taught, was simpler, but it was built of black basalt stone like the rest of the town, and would have included all the necessary requirements of a Synagogue with suitable dignity.

So far, so good. Yet built into it, as we have seen, were these infamous, shameful carved stones. Some of them were Jewish – representations of the Ark of the Covenant, the Manna Pot from which the ancient Hebrews ate while wandering through the desert, the seven-branched candle-stick. Orthodox Jews would have taken exception to those for a start, for as 'graven images' did they not directly contravene the second commandment? In fact, recent excavations in Palestine have unearthed a surprising amount of figurative art in synagogues of Roman times. The great Jewish philosopher Philo had profound sym-pathy with artists, and there is written evidence that images were permitted among some Jews. It doesn't need any imagination to see that there must have been a considerable tension in those days between conservative synagogues who kept to 'the letter of the law' and those who took a much more 'liberal' position. But also, and this is what would have outraged any pious Jew, there were carved and set into the walls the regimental emblem of the 10th Legion of the Roman army, and also the Roman equivalent of the vc. It was as if a brewery installed a neon sign advertising their beer on the wall of a tee-total chapel, or the hammer and sickle were inscribed on Buckingham Palace!

The Jewish attitude to the Roman occupying power ran the gamut of suspicious dislike, through rumbling distrust, all the way to violent and active hatred. Places varied of course. Some villages and towns rubbed along as smoothly as they could; they didn't like them, or what they stood for, but ordinary life had to go on. Other places, like Jerusalem, were always on the edge of explosion; myriads of suspicious eyes were continuously on the lookout for any real or imagined excuse to hit back.

But to have a town like Capernaum, which was so much in the pocket of the Romans as to have their regimental insignia carved on the Synagogue walls; this was a desperately shameful thing for anyone who had any trace of Jewish pride. Disloyal certainly, almost traitorous! How did it happen and why?

The background to these disgraceful stones is told by Luke:

The servant of a certain centurion was so ill that he was going to die, and he was very dear to him. When he heard about Jesus he sent some Jewish elders to him and asked him to come and save his servant's life. They came to Jesus and strenuously urged him to come. 'He is,' they said 'a man who deserves that you should do this for him, for he loves our nation and has himself built us our synagogue.' So Jesus went with them. When he was now quite near the house the centurion sent friends to him. 'Sir,' he said 'do not trouble yourself. I am not worthy that you could come under my roof; nor do I count myself fit to come to you; but just speak a word and my servant will be cured. For I myself am a man under orders, and I have soldiers under me, and I say to one "Go," and he goes; and to another "Come," and he comes; and I say to my servant "Do this," and he does it.' When Jesus heard this he was amazed at him. He turned to the crowd who were following him and said, 'I tell you I have not found such great faith not even in Israel.' And those who had been sent returned to the house and found the servant completely cured.

So this is the explanation of those Roman stones – the building was erected by the centurion. No wonder the elders strenuously urged Jesus to come, they didn't want to upset their patron!

Now this is a rather strange situation. Who was this unusual centurion? Centurions were the highest rank of 'regulars' in the Roman army. Better posts were filled by the civilian nobility on a rota basis, while centurion was the highest rank a regular could hope to attain at the end of his twenty-five years service. So he'd 'risen from the ranks'; he was 'a soldier's soldier', an 'old sweat', and was highly enough regarded to be awarded a very prestigious medal and be put in charge of the garrison at Capernaum.

We don't know his name, but there are several fascinatingly different things about him. First, he was not anti-Jewish. If the Jews in general disliked the Romans, the Romans returned the compliment. The vice of anti-semitism is no new thing, quite apart from the natural dislike any occupying force might feel against a people whom they knew were awaiting any chance to 'do them down', and stab them in the back, they regarded the Jews as 'a filthy race whose religion was a barbarous superstition'. Yet here was an officer in the occupying army building them a Synagogue, not because it was official Roman policy to pacify all the religions of the Empire (which it was), but because he was 'a friend of all Jews'.

He was also out of the ordinary in that he was well aware of Jewish laws and customs. Many riots and commotions were happening because of flat-footed policies and insensitive decisions of Romans who accidentally transgressed Jewish religious laws. No Englishman can be too critical; after all the Indian Mutiny of the nineteenth century was started by ignorant English officers insisting that Indian troops should bite off the cartridge cases, when they were greased by beef fat, and it was against the soldiers' religion to eat beef! This centurion was different, he well understood the situation. We notice that he didn't want Jesus to come to his house in the barracks, and sent friends to stop him. It wasn't because he didn't want to meet him, but because he knew that according to Jewish law it was wrong for a Jew to enter the house of a Gentile, and he didn't want to put Jesus in a difficult situation and in the centre of another controversy.

If you walk into the ruins of the Synagogue today you will see in the open Court, by the side of the main hall, the scratched pattern of a Roman dice game carved into the flagstones of the floor. It is the outline of 'The Kings Game', which it is said the soldiers played after Jesus' trial, using him as an animated 'chess piece'. Yet here they are in the Synagogue courtyard. What were Roman soldiers doing there? Had they been worshipping, they would not have been playing dice. If those scratched outlines date from the right time (and there are others in the Prayer Hall which must have been done long after when the building was derelict) there is at least the remote possibility that they were done by an escort, killing time while their senior officer was in the building. And who were they escorting? Presumably their senior officer, who may even have been this centurion.

Another uncommon thing about this soldier is the care he took over his batman. Centurions were often transferred from unit to unit, and could usually stay in the army long after their minimum twenty-five years service. Presumably a good servant would travel with his master from Legion to Legion. An officer's servant would have been a slave, for the Roman empire was based on slavery.

Normally slaves did not get any consideration once they were old or sick. A Roman authority on farming recommended that every year the farmer should examine his tools and throw out whatever was broken – and do the same with his slaves. Yet far from taking this heartless attitude, Luke tells us that this centurion's servant 'was very dear to him'. One can well imagine that over many years of travels and privations, battles fought, injuries sustained, and perils shared, there would build up between an officer and his batman a mutual liking, respect and care.

Altogether, the centurion comes out of this story as a very remarkable man – a leader of men, certainly, perhaps even a strong disciplinarian, judging by what he said about the way people jumped when he said 'jump', yet caring towards his batman, considerate towards Jesus, and generous towards the Jewish elders.

He was matched on the Jewish side by an equally remarkable man – the Ruler of the Synagogue. He actually allowed the centurion to build the new Synagogue, and even to put carved Roman insignia into it. One can well imagine all the sarcastic comments, and even charges of outright disloyalty from fellow Jews he was laying himself open to. Who was this man? There is no evidence to tell us, but there is one tantalizing possibility. Later in Luke's Gospel he says:

When Jesus came back the crowd welcomed him for they were all waiting for him. A man called Jairus came to him. He was the President of the Synagogue. He threw himself at Jesus' feet and asked him to come to his house, because he had an only daughter who was about twelve years of age and she was dying ... While he was yet speaking someone came from the President's house. 'Your daughter is dead,' he said. 'Don't bother the master any more.' Jesus heard this. 'Don't be afraid,' he said. 'Just have faith and she will be cured.'

When he had come to the house he allowed no one to come in with him, except Peter and John and James, and the girl's father and mother. They were all weeping and wailing for her. 'Stop weeping,' he said, 'for she is not dead but sleeping.' They laughed him down because they were sure she was dead. He took hold of her hand and said to her, 'Child, rise!' Her breath came back to her and immediately she rose. He told them to give her something to eat. Her parents were out of themselves with amazement; but he enjoined them to tell no one what had happened.

Notice that Luke says 'when Jesus came back'. Back to where? There are reasons for assuming that it was back to his home base – Capernaum. And what an impossible request 'tell no one'! How could distraught parents, who had their only daughter miraculously restored to life, keep quiet about it? It was the talk of the town of course, which is how Luke came to hear of it. But, and this is more significant to us, it must have been the talk of the Roman barracks too. What more natural thing can we imagine than when the centurion is chatting to his friend the Ruler of the Synagogue and mentions how worried he is about his batman's health, that he should ask Jairus (if that was his name), 'Do you think Jesus would do something for him?' Or perhaps it was Jairus who suggested it.

The fact that the Jairus story comes after the centurion story in Luke need not worry us. Ever since they were written the stories in the gospels were known as not being in strict chronological order.

So this was the situation Jesus found himself in when he moved to Capernaum. From the Nazareth Synagogue which wouldn't tolerate any suspicion of unorthodoxy, he had changed religious climate completely, to a place where the attitude was very different – tolerant, easy-going, sympathetic. As we have seen, it was the centre of worship in a cosmopolitan crossroads; the people at the Synagogue had 'heard it all, and seen it all'. Jewish teachers of every colour and tradition had passed through, preaching and teaching on their way. Like all such mixed and mobile churches, they'd learned to accommodate themselves to various views, accept everything with 'a pinch of salt', listen with amused detachment to the sometimes extreme or eccentric views of their guests, and make the best of them. To tell the truth, the people at the Capernaum Synagogue were rather pleased with themselves; they were active, theologically tolerant, politically aware of the realities – in their opinion just the kind of group their God would appreciate in heaven!

It was just this Synagogue that Jesus deliberately chose as his headquarters. Of all the places he could have gone to, he chose Capernaum. 'Here they will listen', he must have reasoned. 'However startling my teaching is, here I will get a fair hearing: here they will take my message of the Kingdom seriously.' Jesus chose Capernaum for several reasons, not least because of the kind of Synagogue it had.

And so it happened that in this small town, inside the stone walls of the Capernaum Synagogue, and looked down on by the Roman regimental insignia, the beginnings of the Christian Gospel was preached. In this small area he told parables, performed miracles of healing, and argued with religious scholars. There was no danger of riots or assassination attempts here.

Not only this, but here Jesus began to organize his followers, calling them away from their daily work, training them, leading them out on preaching expeditions, and eventually sending them out on their own. Sometimes they were away for days, sometimes weeks, and, possibly once, for several months. Yet always they came 'home', to where they kept their old clothes, where family and friends lived, and where the Synagogue authorities were always pleased to see them.

But it all went sour. The grand hopes and the lofty aspirations fell flat, the fresh beginnings and the flourishing start led to nothing. Why? What happened? Perhaps we can find a clue in the account of one of Jesus' sermons in John's gospel. Jesus said:

> 'The bread which I will give him is my flesh, which is given that the world may have life.' So the Jews argued with each other. 'How,' they said, 'can this man give us his flesh to eat?' Jesus said to them: 'This is the truth I tell you – unless you eat the flesh of the Son of Man and drink his blood, you cannot possess eternal life within yourselves. He who eats my flesh and drinks my blood has eternal life, and I will raise him up on the last day . . .'
>
> He said these things when he was teaching in the Synagogue at Capernaum. When they had heard this discourse many of his disciples said: 'This word is hard! Who is able to listen to it? . . . After this many of his disciples turned back and would not walk with him any more.

Now John, writing many years later, from the background of the early church, where the sharing of the bread and wine representing the body and blood of Christ was the centre of their worship, obviously sees the symbolical significance of that sermon. How far what John records is a verbatim record of what was said depends on one's view of the Bible, but there's no doubt that for the listeners on the spot at the time what Jesus said on that day was something that they were either for or against – they couldn't be neutral about it!

Here was Jesus claiming to have a unique relationship with God, and thereby forcing judgment! Interestingly, the Greek word for judgment is 'krisis'. Either he was right, or he was wrong. With all the other visiting preachers to their Synagogue, they could nod knowingly and keep an open mind, but not this one! Now now! Jesus had put them in the most exquisitely uncomfortable position they knew, where they had to make up their mind. They either had to accept him, or reject him, it was all or nothing, and Jesus left them no fence in between to sit on.

It was then that Jesus realized the price which has to be paid for urbane tolerance, for the advantages of that Synagogue were at the same time its disadvantages. They were not willing to change! Their minds were open – but at both ends. Granted there were great crowds who followed Jesus, but they only followed him because he was the latest sensation, not because they were willing to make his demanding teaching their own. They looked for signs and wonders, not sacrifice and salvation. There were some individuals of course, who left everything to follow, and whose names are still remembered nearly 2,000 years afterwards, but there was no sign of a great groundswell of dedication to the Kingdom Jesus preached.

In the end Jesus despaired of them. Of Chorazin, a village two miles from Capernaum, and of Bethsaida, a short boat journey away, he said:

'if the mighty works done in you have been done in the despised Greek cities of Tyre and Sidon, they would long ago have sat in dust and ashes and repented. And as for you Capernaum, will you be exalted to heaven? You'll be hurtled to hell, for he who sets no value on me, sets no value on him who sent me.'

What seems to have angered Jesus was that their very civilized tolerance proved to be as firm a barrier to his teaching as the outright opposition shown in Nazareth. A doorway can be blocked just as securely with flexible and soft netting as it can with sharp barbed wire. An idea can be killed just as surely with apathy as with opposition. Mildly interested detachment will only take people so far. There come occasions when it has to turn into dedicated commitment, and Capernaum wasn't ready to do that.

In all conscience the situation was dire enough, the country was seething with resentment and rebellion, and it was only a matter of time before it broke out. Any realist could see that it was doomed to failure, yet there was an awful inevitability about the future carnage and horror. Relationships between village and village, town and town, were fragile, allegiances changed quickly, and once reliable friends could easily descend on you during the night to massacre and plunder.

In this context Jesus taught about a new kingdom, a radically different order of priorities. Writ large this could really change society. In this framework he healed broken, dead people, and offered healing to the broken and dead world. Against this background he cast out demons, and was ready to cast out the devils who threatened to drop the nation into the fires of hell. In place of the violent prejudices, the sterile policies, and the corruption of a society which was clearly disintegrating, he offered a new kingdom, a new context in which personal holiness and happiness could be found, and the political and social problems of society could be eased.

But the people in Capernaum offered him only a semi-detached faith, a luke-warm sceptical response, an academic argument. Real, self-sacrificing people like Jesus and his followers were admired – but only at a distance.

It wouldn't do then, and it won't do now! It is as foolish

and disastrous as the level-crossing keeper who was sacked from the railway after he opened only one of the level crossing gates, because he 'half-expected a train'.

Our twentieth century cannot afford to be too critical of those Capernaum people of the first. We live in a world where we can invent a computer that does millions of complicated sums in a split second, yet we cannot think of a way to ensure that everyone has enough to eat. We can take photographs of remote planets and comets, yet we torture and murder our own fellow human beings. We can invent new substances that nature has never thought of, yet cannot find a way of removing the shadow of the mushroom cloud that could easily destroy us all. And we, too, offer him interested detachment!

As one travels round the shores of Galilee today, the sites of these places are overgrown, derelict, depopulated. While other places have been built upon, and rebuilt many times, these places have not. Indeed, even the precise sites of some have been forgotten. The archaeologists have a clear field in which to delve and dig, as they are doing now in Capernaum, and where just a few years ago they dug up the shameful stones of the Synagogue.

They are genuinely shameful stones. For a Jew they were shameful because they meant a 'sell-out' to the Romans. The Christian sees a more sophisticated shame in them – the shame of a people who had ears to hear but did not hear, who had eyes to see but did not see, who had personal experience of a saviour, but did not respond.

5

Parlez-Vous Aramaic?

What languages did he speak?

Most of us are lost in admiration of people who have the gift of languages – it goes beyond just a retentive memory, the ability to mimic sounds accurately, and an almost musical ear for cadences. There are people who can speak a whole handful of different languages with what seems like effortless ease. Henri Schmidt, of (appropriately) the Terminology Department of the United Nations, admitted that he could only speak nineteen languages because he hadn't time to 'brush' up another twelve, and George Campbell of the BBC Overseas Service worked with thirty-nine.

The majority of people, especially in England, find it very difficult to learn any other language, and wonder why on earth they should! But one only has to cross the North Sea to Holland, to meet a people, almost all of whom speak two languages, most three, and many four. Dutch is what they were brought up on, English is vital and most of their television programmes are in English (or 'American'), German and French are also very common. Dutch children are expected to spend a great deal of their time in school learning languages, and they do it very successfully. I have visited Holland several times, and only ever met one Dutch person who could not speak English.

This facility of theirs clearly comes from hard work and prolonged educational effort, yet it would be wrong to think that it is always attained by academic achievement. In fairly undeveloped parts of the world there are many different languages and dialects in close proximity. In Ghana, for example, there are dozens of different languages and dialects, and it is common for the average uneducated villager to speak his own tongue, the language of the tribe next-door, and in addition have enough English to 'get by'. They achieve this, not by prolonged schooling, but by having their broadcasting in seven languages, and by the normal ways of trade, and work. After all, if you go somewhere else to work where they speak a different language, you have to learn it – fast.

So when we ask the question 'How many languages did Jesus and the disciples speak?' we are not asking how educated they were but how many languages would they have picked up and used as part of their daily lives. This is a complicated question which experts are still studying, but the provisional answers are most surprising.

Let us start with the most obvious and common – Aramaic. A very ancient language, it was the common speech of the Assyrian Empire in the eighth century BC when it was used in diplomacy, implying that it was understood over a very wide area. It was the language the Jewish exiles had to learn when they were deported to Babylon, and still persisted over a wide area of the Near East in Jesus' time. It survived because it was adaptable, over the years it incorporated words from whatever culture held sway over the area, and it proved to be a useful multi-purpose language. The authors of Daniel and Ezra in the Old Testament, writing about 400 BC composed half their books in it. It was the lingua franca from the Mediterranean to India, and from Asia Minor to Egypt. All scholars accept that by the time of Jesus it was the most common language of ordinary Jewish people in Palestine; it would have been Aramaic they used in normal conversation.

Great excitement was caused in 1947 by the discovery of the Dead Sea Scrolls, buried in caves by the Essenes, which when they were examined showed that many of their manuscripts were written in Aramaic. This is typical of almost the whole country – from bits of broken pottery which were used to write little notes in ancient days, inscriptions on the earthenware pots in which they used to store the bones of the dead, from IOUs, bills, deeds and letters – all indicate that Aramaic was a far more popular language among the people of Palestine than Hebrew.

It is clear too that it was the language that Jesus used a great deal. The Gospel of Mark is interesting in this connection, for it is written in very bad Greek. It is a document written in Greek by a man who didn't know the language very well, and *thought in Aramaic*. He proves this several times by quoting the Aramaic words that Jesus used, and then translating them for his readers; such as:

He said '*Talitha Koum!*' (which means 'little girl I say to you "get up"').

With a deep sigh he said to him '*Ephphatha!*' (which means 'be opened').

'*Abba*,' father, he said.

And of course there is the agonizing cry from the cross, which has echoed down the centuries – it is interesting that when Jesus was driven down to his innermost soul, to his innermost extremity – he spoke in Aramaic.

'*Eloi, Eloi, lama sabachthani?*' – which means 'My God, my God, why have you forsaken me?'

So we are on safe ground in assuming that Jesus spoke Aramaic fluently, for Mark records some of the actual words, quite apart from the general historical evidence. In fact, a dialect of Aramaic is still used in worship by the

Syrian Orthodox Church, and can be heard at their services – the sounds of it are harmonious and pleasing to the ear, there are few harsh consonants, or unattractive vowels, especially when spoken in a Galilean accent.

For instance, put into English lettering, this is how the first five lines of the Lord's Prayer would have sounded when Jesus first taught it to the disciples:

Abun d'bashmayo	Our Father in heaven
Netkadash shmockh,	Holy be your name
tite malkutockh,	Your Kingdom come,
nehwe sebyonockh	Your will be done
aykanod'bashmayo	On earth as in heaven.
of bar'o.	

Which brings us to the second most popular language of the country in those days, Greek. The big influx of Greek into Palestine was when Alexander the Great, the king of Macedon, conquered the area in 332 BC, and included it in his huge, but short-lived empire. It then became government policy to use it everywhere from official business to conversation among the educated. Greek pottery of the sixth century BC has been dug up in Palestine, and several inscriptions in Greek have survived dating from 217 BC onwards. There seems to be little point in setting up inscriptions in public places, unless at least some of the people could read them.

One fascinating collection of eight pieces of broken pottery used as notes has been found from what was obviously a money-lending establishment. They are reminders of how much had been lent to particular individuals, and even a receipt from a borrower for thirty-five drachmas. Of these eight notes, six are in Aramaic, one in Greek and one in both. Dating from 277 BC, these show that in Palestine, although Aramaic was the commonest language, the use of Greek was increasing.

The most conclusive evidence comes, however, from burial pots dating to about the time of Jesus. It was the custom in those days to place bodies in burial chambers, and after one year remove the bones, which would then be put in wooden or pottery containers called Ossuaries, to be reburied. Many of these ossuaries have been excavated, or discovered in disused caves, and naturally, they usually have funerary inscriptions and names scratched on them. Out of 194 inscribed ossuaries on record, twenty six per cent are in Aramaic or Hebrew, nine per cent in Greek and Aramaic or Hebrew, and sixty-four per cent are in Greek alone. This could indicate that Greek was comfortably overtaking Aramaic and Hebrew, at least in certain areas of Palestine.

So did Jesus speak Greek? We cannot be conclusively sure, but it is quite possible, even probable that he did. Consider for example the story that Mark tells of the time when Jesus seems to have decided to 'get away from it all', and leave the Galilee area completely. He went to 'the borders of Tyre and Sidon', and tried to hide himself away in the house of an unknown woman. Many see this episode as a major turning-point in the ministry of Jesus. It could have been the point when Jesus decided to broaden his ministry from the Jews of his homeland, to the Gentiles of the lands surrounding Palestine, so foreshadowing the appeal of the gospel to the whole world. If one takes Mark's account of the ministry, it is possible to see Jesus more or less abandoning Galilee, and from this point concentrating on Greek speaking areas outside the dominions of Herod Antipas.

Perhaps on the other hand, he did this because of growing opposition, for there are indications of secret visits to Galilee, and hurried escapes, from this point onwards. Whichever way it was, he was fulfilling his ministry in Greek areas, and probably, therefore, had a working knowledge of the language.

He went into a house and he did not wish anyone to know about it, but he could not be there without people knowing about it. When a woman whose daughter had an unclean spirit heard about him, she immediately came and threw herself at his feet. The woman was a Greek, a Syrophoenician by birth. She asked him to cast the demon out of her daughter . . .

In this story Jesus is in Gentile country, and by describing the woman as 'Greek' Mark means that she was educated and Greek speaking. So although Jesus and the disciples would normally have spoken Aramaic, they clearly were sufficiently acquainted with the Greek language to be able to hold a normal conversation in it. Indeed, as we shall see later, there was even quick-fire repartee, which shows considerable fluency.

It is only fair, however, to note that Matthew also tells this story, only in his version the woman is a 'Canaanite', and the Canaanites were ancestral enemies of the Jews. The moral of the story for Matthew was that the message of Jesus applies not only to the Jews themselves but to everyone else as well. A Canaanite woman would, presumably have spoken Aramaic, and bearing in mind where she lived, Greek as well. However, in the choice between Mark's and Matthew's versions there would be good grounds for choosing Mark as the earliest written, and more likely to be accurate.

Not only this, but there are other stories of Jesus visiting districts where Greek would be the prevailing language. Take, for instance, the eerie story of the Gadarene swine. This happened on the other side of the Lake of Galilee in the area known as The Decapolis. In the three Gospel versions of the story, Jesus is visiting a wierd place – a graveyard haunted by evil spirits, and lived in by a naked maniac who had superhuman strength (Matthew says there were two of them). The episode took place within the territory of Gadera, one of the ten cities of the Decapolis, itself an important Greek city noted for its temples, theatres and warm baths, which came within the province of Syria. Speaking Greek, they bore considerable animosity towards the Jews, whole-heartedly adopted Greek culture and Greek buildings, and, of course, kept pigs, which was against Jewish religious laws. 'And the pig . . . it is unclean for you. You must not eat their meat or touch their carcases.' An interesting side-light is that when Jesus was telling the story of The Prodigal Son, and described how the lad went to 'a far country' he must have been thinking of a non-Jewish, Greek-speaking area, for the only job the down-and-out boy could eventually find, was feeding pigs.

In the conversation Jesus had with the man which language did he use? It could have been Aramaic, but it is more likely to have been Greek.

Another instance is in John's Gospel, when he records Jesus immediately after entering Jerusalem on the first Palm Sunday making a speech to the crowds. In what he says, Jesus predicts his own death, but the reason for making the speech at all is because: 'There were some Greeks among those who went up to worship at the Feast. They came to Philip, who was from Bethsaida in Galilee, with a request. "Sir," they said, "we would like to see Jesus." Philip went to tell Andrew, and Andrew and Philip in turn told Jesus.'

Now if the words that Jesus is recorded to have said were actually said to the Greeks who had asked to meet him, it seems obvious that Jesus must have spoken in Greek.

So to try to sum up: though it cannot be proved, the evidence seems to point to the fact that Jesus and some of the disciples, at least those who were used to trade and commerce, like Peter and Matthew, had enough command of the Greek language to hold normal conversations.

There is also reason for thinking that Jesus knew a third language – Hebrew. This ancient tongue certainly dates back to the twelfth century BC, earlier than Aramaic, and both battled it out for supremacy for over a thousand years. One sixth-century BC incident is recorded in the Old Testament, when the Assyrian King Sennacherib sent a messenger to King Hezekiah in Jerusalem, and he threw threats at the Jews in the conversation which took place below the city walls with all the people looking on. 'So Hezekiah's representatives said "please speak to us in Aramaic, since we understand it. Don't speak to us in Hebrew in the hearing of the people on the wall."'

However, it didn't work – Sennacherib's field commander was not appointed to his job for nothing, and proceeded to shout out his threats in Hebrew, with the precise aim of frightening everyone within earshot.

Over the following centuries Hebrew gradually declined as a normal spoken language among ordinary people. But its hold, though slackening, was tenacious and long-lasting. When Alexander's dominion over the Near East gave Greek a tremendous boost, Hebrew and Aramaic still persisted. Many of the Dead Sea Scrolls are written in Hebrew, and show that at the time of Jesus it was still a language in common religious use. It is possible that there were particular families, or communities, where it was a cause for pride that they never lost command of their ancient tongue, and where Hebrew was the usual spoken language.

Scholars are still arguing as to whether Hebrew was a live spoken language at the time, or whether it was a dead language studied and used as a second written language, much as Latin was in England up to recent times. However, on the whole we can with some confidence assume that it was a fairly common spoken language, because of those ossuary pots mentioned earlier. In a store of them dating to Jesus' time, discovered on the Mount of Olives, many are inscribed with Hebrew words, 'Martha our Mother', 'Salome the proselyte', 'John the craftsman' and so on. As these inscriptions were intended for the family to read, and often are not neat carvings, but just quick scratchings, we can infer that Hebrew was the ordinary language those families used.

In the excavations going on at the Temple Mount in Jerusalem, various inscriptions have been dug up. They are written in Hebrew and meant to be read by the people attending the Temple. There have also been found inscribed stones written in Greek, saying in effect 'Gentiles keep out'. It is no surprise that Hebrew should be used in worship and the religious activities of the Jewish people, for it was regarded by them as a holy language, the true speech of God's Chosen People; but it was more than that – it had a patriotic element to it as well.

So did Jesus speak Hebrew? To answer this we have to know how the Synagogue services of his day were organized. Basically, there were three parts to the service, first prayer, then the reading of scripture, then followed teaching. For the genius of the Synagogue system was that it was a teaching centre. There was no full-time minister or preacher. The President of the Synagogue could choose seven people to read scripture passages, and invite anyone he thought fit to give the teaching. The seven readers would be presented with the scrolls of scripture *written in ancient Hebrew* and would read from them. As many of the congregation might not have understood the Hebrew it was common practice for a Synagogue official to translate it into Aramaic or Greek, one verse at a time in the case of the first five books of the Old Testament, three verses at a time for the rest. Now consider the story Luke tells.

So Jesus came to Nazareth ... and as was his habit, he went into the Synagogue on the Sabbath day, and he stood up to read the lesson. The roll of the prophet Isaiah was given to him. He opened the roll and found the passage where it is written ...

The fact that what Jesus said on that occasion caused uproar does not concern us here, but rather that he read the Hebrew roll of Isaiah. The only story of his youth which survives shows that he was a keen student of religious matters, and through the accounts of his ministry in Galilee we know that he often spoke and preached in the Synagogues around the area. He may or may not have used Hebrew as a spoken tongue, but it is certain that he could read it.

This gives Jesus the knowledge of three languages. Aramaic, Greek and Hebrew, probably in that order of fluency. There is a possibility that he may have had a nodding acquaintance with a fourth – Latin.

This was the official language of the Roman occupying power, and though it never gained any ground outside Roman spheres of influence, it was used in legal matters, put on milestones, and on inscriptions which the officials were only too ready to erect. Several of these Latin stones have been discovered, the most intriguing was found a few years ago at Caesarea Maritime, the military capital of the country in Roman times. Sceptics have tended in the past to disparage the gospels by pointing to the fact that no evidence that Pontius Pilate was in Palestine existed apart from the gospel stories themselves. However, recently a badly mutilated inscription has been found at Caesarea that actually mentions him. It seems to be part of a plaque on a temple or public building.

> ... the Tiberium
> ... Pontius Pilatus
> ... (Pref)ect of Judaea.

This stone is interesting in itself, but notice that it is written in Latin.

Jesus's first trials before the Jewish authorities would probably have been held in Hebrew or Aramaic, for reasons of patriotic pride. But what language did Pilate use when Jesus was referred to him? That Pilate, a career administrator pushed on by an ambitious wife, should bother to learn either Hebrew or Aramaic during his ten years in charge of the territory is highly unlikely. He made no attempt to understand the Jewish culture and susceptibilities or to accommodate himself to them, so there is little chance that he would have put himself out to learn what he would doubtless have called a 'barbarous tongue'. He would have spoken Greek for choice, and Latin for business, and so we can guess that Jesus' last trial was probably held in Greek.

At the conclusion of these terrible proceedings, Jesus was led forth to crucifixion preceded by a man holding a placard. In cases like this they always went the long way round, passing through as many streets as possible. This was not just as a deterrent to crime, but so that anyone who had any evidence which could acquit the prisoner could come forward and demand a re-trial. If no one did, the sentence was carried out, and the placard was nailed to the top of the cross. In Jesus' case the notice read 'The King of the Jews' according to Mark; 'This is Jesus the King of the Jews' according to Matthew; 'This is the King of the Jews' says Luke; and 'Jesus of Nazareth, the King of the Jews' records John. All very much the same, and typical of the way that different eye-witnesses vary slightly in what they remember. But John goes further: 'It was written in Hebrew, and in Latin, and in Greek.' Hebrew for Jewish people, Latin because it was a legal matter, and Greek for the foreigners who at festival time crammed the city – Pilate covered the lot. Barclay sees in this mixture a parable for the time, the three great languages, representing the contributions of three great peoples to civilization. The Hebrew of the Jewish nation who taught religion to the world, the Latin of the empire which led the world in law and order, and the Greek of the civilization which showed the world the noblest beauty of form and thought. So the last hours of Jesus' life was a babel of different languages, in each of them he is proclaimed king. And as for Aramaic, the speech of the uneducated peasant, it clearly wasn't considered significant enough to be on the official placard, but it was what Jesus used on the cross, the speech of his last moments, his 'home' language.

It has been common enough to regard Jesus as a man who lived a basic life in a remote backwater of the world; who taught a great but simple message to an ignorant people; and was not caught up in the complexities of life, or the conundrums of civilization. This view is much too naive, for Jesus lived at a time of clashing confrontation in the melting pot of the world. Political rebellion, cultural instability, economic oppression, all washed over him, affected him, and coloured what he had to say. It also, of course, dictated the languages in which he said it.

6

The Happy Breeze

Jesus the humourist

An old Jewish store-keeper was on his death bed. With his last breaths he whispered: 'Miriam, my dear wife, are you there?' 'Yes, my dear,' came the reply. 'Reuben, my eldest son, are you there?' 'Yes, father,' 'Levi, my second son, are you there too?' 'Yes, father.' 'David, my youngest son, are you there?' 'Yes, father.' 'Deborah, my prettiest daughter, are you there?' 'Yes, father.' 'Ruth, my youngest daughter, are you there?' 'Yes, father.' After a short pause for thought, and with superhuman effort, the old man sat bolt upright in bed, with his white hair dishevelled, and shouted 'Then who's looking after the shop already?'

This typical Jewish joke has a macabre quality, and is based on modern conceptions of Jewish people as tradesmen, but as Jewish people have fulfilled different roles in various communities down the centuries, so the settings and the jokes have changed. There must have been many others about, say, Jewish farmers, bureaucrats, and moneylenders. In Galilee two thousand years ago, when nearly the whole of life was run by Jews, the setting of the humour was universal and every situation was grist to the mill. Nothing was immune to having its leg pulled, and its absurdities exposed with a mighty blast of laughter.

Yet was there a particular 'note' in this humour? Was

there then, as there is now, a special Jewish style of joke which shows hints in the New Testament? Did the tragic background of strife, suffering, and discrimination of Jesus' time, release itself in a humour with a identifiable colour and accent, as it has done since? 'Nonsense' some people have said, 'apart from word-play and puns which are limited to a particular language, humour is basically the same world-wide and history-deep.'

Whatever is the truth of it, one cannot imagine that Jesus did not have a sense of humour, for laughter is part of what it is to be human, and must have bubbled through his life as much as through everyone else's since the world began. To picture him as always mild in manner, endlessly patient, grave in speech, and serious and unsmiling to the point of being dour is a sign of someone who hasn't read the Gospels recently enough, carefully enough, or sympathetically enough. Harry Emerson Fosdick said of the Jesus he saw in the New Testament: 'He often lets the ripple of a happy breeze play over the surface of his mighty deep.'

Nevertheless, trying to identify examples of his laughter and wit is extremely difficult. Not only is it the death of humour to try to define it and take it apart, but the search is bedevilled by the worthy attempts of his pious followers ever since to take in deadly seriousness every word he said. For example, once Jesus said lightly, that when we give to charitable causes we shouldn't blow a trumpet to announce the fact, a plain enough use of humorous exaggeration to make the point. That didn't stop an eminent New Testament scholar writing, 'I have not found, though I have searched for it long and seriously, even the least mention of a trumpet in almsgiving.' It was a joke, for heaven's sake!

What is more significant, by not recognizing humour when we see it, and by taking every word literally, it is possible to distort what Jesus actually said, particularly when he used the 'humour of opposites', and build great theological principles the wrong way round on what was meant to be light-hearted comment.

What religious people often did not, and we might as well admit, sometimes still do not see, is that tragedy and comedy compliment and strengthen each other. When logic reaches the infinite paradox of God it turns into a joke, and the laughing face and the crying face are seen to be two sides of the same Godhead. The 'Man of Sorrows' only rings true in eternity if he is at the same time the 'Divine Comedian'. There is an Irish proverb which underlines the perils of solemnity when it says that we can pray ourselves into heaven, but if we pray too hard we can pray ourselves out the other side!

This tendency to being over-literal and humourless has affected the records of what Jesus said, and the Gospels as we have them now. In the thirty years or so before they were systematically written down, his sayings were re-membered and treasured, and in an age when learning 'by rote' and with surprising accuracy was the norm, we can justifiably assume faithful transmission of much of what Jesus said. But most of the humour was lost in the translation from Aramaic to Greek, and what could not be handed on even by the best memory was the smile on his face, the playful intonation, the wink, or the whimsical expression in his eyes. It wasn't only the stories he told, it was 'the way he told them' which was part of what he was in fact saying.

Providentially, the very carefulness with which the early Christians remembered his sayings accidently preserved at least some of the humour, even when they had lost sight of the joke. So we have in Matthew, Mark and Luke, (though not, interestingly, in John) glimpses of a light-hearted Jesus oddly wrapped in solemn speeches, and isolated comments preserved in unusual situations. Obviously, those who remembered them couldn't think why he said some of these things in the way he did, but put it in because that's what he did say.

So, however difficult it is now at the end of this process, it is nevertheless possible, even two thousand years afterwards, to search for and recognize touches of his humour shining through the cracks in the stories.

First, there is a difference between a genuine good humour, and someone who cracks clever jokes at the expense of others. Jesus was one of the first kind – a genial person, whe rejected the kill-joy, and was happily regarded as an asset to a party and a feast, otherwise people would not have invited him. The many times Jesus alluded to marriage feasts and associated the Kingdom of God with wining and dining in heaven clearly means that he enjoyed them. All the indications show that he had not only humour but 'good humour', the ability to raise an sociable smile, as well as an outright laugh.

More than this, as we shall see, he was also a witty man who appreciated and responded to the wit in others. Whether Jesus ever told funny stories for their own sake, as we do today, is impossible to tell, for naturally enough, the Gospel writers concerned as they were with communicating the message, didn't record them. The humour we see traces of now is nearly all directed, purposeful, and aimed at communicating truth as Jesus saw it.

The root of his humour was paradox, which is one of the deepest forms. Jesus' teaching is full of it, and he throws in metaphor after metaphor, bringing together wildly inappropriate things, the most unlikely illustrations, and showing with a hint of humour, that they are, after all, the same. There is a vast difference between salt, light, and yeast, yet we can sense a playfulness in Jesus as he shows that each of them can only function by spending

71

or losing itself. The ultimate paradox is when he acted the parable of breaking the bread at his last meal, using the most ordinary to express the unique, and went on to win by losing, to live by dying, to become a victor by being a victim. Beneath the suffering is a deep and knowing smile.

Though Jesus used many kinds of humour, the most commonly preserved is a sharp irony. What saved it from turning into sarcasm was that there was no cracking of a good joke regardless of who got hurt. In the story of the people who give to charity and let everyone know, the humour is not only in the reference to trumpets but in the punch-line, 'they have their reward'. In other words, 'watch out for what you want, you might get it!' The same moral comes out when he tells his followers not to look miserable in religious matters. 'Some people try to look dismal, and they have their reward, they succeed!'

There is fun in being outrageous, as Jesus knew. A yoke was regarded by everyone as a hateful thing meaning servitude and slavery, and even the prophets said so. So it is not 'in spite' of this but because of this that Jesus said with a shocking ease 'Take my yoke upon you.' When he was talking to priests he told them, 'the harlots go into the kingdom of God before you!' This had the clear intention to shock. If we think about it, he had to have a smile on his face, to show that he recognized the enormity of what he had said.

This element of the preposterous comes out when he talked about the man who went around with a plank in his eye, offering to help other people who had splinters in theirs. It also appears with the Pharisees who 'swallowed a camel but "gagged" at a gnat'. When he told someone to 'let the dead bury the dead' the vision of a dead undertaker still at work is patently absurd. 'Don't throw pearls before swine' is deliberate overstatement, for no one in their right senses would do any such thing, let alone a Jew, but that in fact enhances a grotesque and memorable saying.

One example of overstatement is well-known. When Jesus told his listeners not to worry so much, he used as illustrations the birds and flowers who manage perfectly well without storage cupboards and savings accounts. Clearly, he was not saying that his listeners should avoid any sensible forward planning at all, though this is literally what it says, but by exaggeration making the point that over-preoccupation with the future is a God-denying view of the present. Not to see the exaggeration is to miss the twinkle in his eye, and lose our sense of proportion.

Incidentally, as part of this story there is recorded a brief sentence about the futility of a person who worried about living an hour longer, a wonderful starting point for a laughable and ironic story, which if it was originally told as a parable could have gone on for a long time with a punch-line that is now lost.

Another aspect of Jesus' lighthearted approach is the way he gave his closest disciples nicknames, and those nicknames were sometimes the direct opposite of what the people were like. He called James and John 'Sons of Thunder'. Whether that meant that they were loud noisy characters, or that they were the opposite, quiet and retiring, we don't know. Nowadays, we can quite easily call someone who is as bald as a billiard ball 'Curly', and a sixteen-stone roly-poly 'Slim'. Clearly this is what Jesus did when on a visit to Caesarea Philippi, he renamed Simon 'Cephas,' (Rocky) which was just about the most improbable name he could think of. Simon was probably the most unstable person among the Twelve. He alternated between impetuous devotion and ox-like stupidity, he was capable of trying disastrously to walk on water in an excess of religious zeal and lying cowardice at the trial of Jesus. 'China-shop Bill' would have fitted him, for anyone less stable and durable as a rock would be hard to find. Which is precisely why Jesus used it as a nickname.

The laughter was turned into a deeper joy over the years, when Peter grew into his name, and what started as a joke turned into a redeeming fact.

We can spot humour in what Jesus said when Peter, insensitive as ever, started to run through all he'd given up to follow him. 'Really?' Jesus replies in effect, 'All right then, Peter, I promise you for immediate delivery, a hundred times what you've given up; a hundred houses, a hundred wives, a hundred lots of children, and a hundred mothers-in-law! See how you like that!'

In addition, like all expert communicators, he must have known and used humour as the acid that can eat away prejudice and bigotry when all other methods fail. Once when Jesus was arguing with the Pharisees he congratulated them in mock admiration: 'You've made an excellent job — — — of completely nullifying the command of God.' Notice how the Gospel writer preserved the words, but lost the pause, and thereby missed the humour. If we restore the timing, we see the joke.

The great chance Jesus had in using humour was in his parables. In the Gospels we have poor filleted versions of what the original stories must have been like. As they were told they must have been long, colourful tales, full of drama, dialogue, tension and humour, things impossible to remember and retell thirty years later. What we have now are only the compressed bones of the plots. But even so, there are small touches of the original humour that can still be found. For instance the punchline of the parable of the wineskins is often overlooked. Jesus tells how it is stupid to rip a piece of cloth off a new coat in order to patch an old one, and just as silly to put new and still fementing wine into old and hardened wine skins. They would crack and both skins and wine would be lost. The moral is that Jesus can't put his new teaching into the old religious structures. But then he goes on to say: 'And

74

no one after drinking old wine wants the new, for he says "The old is better."' So Jesus is saying that people don't like change, are basically conservative, and much prefer the comfort of what they are used to. People don't like new wine with the strange rough taste, or wearing new coats when the old one was nicely 'worn in'. He doesn't even expect people to like what he says or does! So this self-depreciating and sardonic aside at the end of the parable which is missed by so many, is a punch-line that adds a completely new message to the whole story.

There is one glorious bit of humour, which we can be certain Jesus would not have been able to resist. It must have 'gone missing' somewhere along the line. It occurs in the Parable of the Good Samaritan. Suppose that the traveller was in fact an orthodox Jew, travelling on the road from Jerusalem to Jericho because he wanted to get to Galilee without having to go through Samaria. It took longer, but it was worth it because he wouldn't run the risk of mixing with that despised race. And who came and helped him? The Samaritan!

A sense of humour is a dangerous thing, however; it is risky because people without a sense of humour may take it literally and get tied in knots as a result. Such a thing has happened with the parable of the Unjust Steward. It is the story of the manager who knew that he was going to be sacked for incompetence, so when he was clearing up his affairs went to each of his boss's debtors and halved all their debts so that when he finally left he had grateful people to go to. The boss found out about his fraud and, surprisingly, commended him. Taken literally, this parable could be used to justify a worldly church filled with sharp, unscrupulous and fraudulent operators. Theologians have turned and squirmed to draw respectable morals out of it and have failed to be convincing, particularly as immediately after it Luke puts a saying of Jesus that is directly opposed to everything it stands for.

It is a good yarn, of course, it's clever and contains surprises, but the only reasonable explanation for it is that Jesus was being funny, and designed it to be transparently opposite to what he meant. Elton Trueblood in his book *The Humor of Christ* lists thirty instances of Jesus' humour, and says of this parable:

> Christ is saying in effect, that if the disciples want to get ahead, they would be wise to cheat in a big way and not fool around with a little. Don't steal *from* the bank, he suggests, steal the bank, and then, instead of being punished, you will be respected.

This is the nearest the New Testament gets to telling a story for the sake of it. The humour lies, as everyone present at the time must have appreciated, in the incongruity of who was telling it to whom.

One or two of Jesus' 'throw-away remarks' have survived the centuries and show again the wry way he had of pointing-up opposites. One occurred at the Last Supper: 'The kings of the Gentiles lord it over them; and those who exercise authority over them call themselves Benefactors.' Now if ever there was a word to describe the general run of kings and emperors in the first-century world it wasn't 'benefactors'; tyrants, barbarians, brutes, yes, but if they called themselves 'benefactors' it was a sick joke. Now this phrase 'they call themselves benefactors' is completely gratuitous, doesn't lead to anything, adds nothing to the point that Jesus was making, and the speech makes just as good sense without it. It was a humorous remark, made because Jesus thought of it at the time, and has no other justification than a smiling and ironic aside.

The Gospels are in fact very short of dialogue, and retell

very little of it. Which makes it difficult to spot the quick-fire sally, and reply. But we have one surviving account of how he reacted to the wit of other people in the story of the Syro-Phoenician woman. We saw in a previous chapter that the conversation may well have been in Greek, for it occurred when Jesus and the disciples were in a foreign country that bordered Galilee. Of the two versions of what happened the oldest, Mark, preserves the humour best.

Jesus thinks his primary mission is to his own country-men, though he clearly regards Gentiles and Samaritans as just as needy and responsive, he wants to concentrate his work on the Jews. So when lying low over the border either for rest or to escape danger, he is not well pleased when a Greek woman recognizes him and makes a fuss on behalf of her sick daughter. Jesus answers her plea with a bantering epigram, probably known to both of them. '"First let the children eat all they want," he told her, "for it is not right to take the children's bread and toss it to their little dogs."' Immediately the woman picks up the analogy and replies: '"Yes Lord, but even the pet dogs under the table get the children's crumbs."' In other words, 'all right, we Gentiles may be dogs, but even dogs get fed, and I don't want anything special – can't I even have the bits you throw away?' Jesus is clearly impressed by her wit and her persistence, and warmed to her: '"For this reply you may go; the demon has left your daughter."' It is inconceivable that at this pointed 'come-back' Jesus did not laugh, or at the very least smile. In fact one of the best proofs of Jesus' wit is the way he responded to the wit of someone else.

If ever a poet got it wrong it was Swinburne who wrote;

Thou hast conquered, O pale Galilean,
The world has grown grey with Thy breath.

Jesus certainly conquered the Roman Empire, and has made his way into the hearts of a quarter of the world's population, but he has done it not in grey solemnity, but in the lively mirth of people like the Franciscans who had to be reproved for laughing in church; the Friars whose knock-about jokes preserved the mediaeval church from fossilization; Wesley's circuit riders who were renowned as the best funny-story tellers of the age; and Salvationists whose earthy and holy hilarity blew the dirt from their hearts.

Swinburne obviously forgot that the New Testament starts with angelic rejoicing over the birth of a baby, ends with mighty choirs singing Hallelujah Choruses, and in between tells the story of an amazing person who refused to fast on Mondays and Thursdays because he was on a continuous honeymoon with his followers, told people that his work of 'finding lost people' was the happiest in the world, and had as one of his favourite words 'rejoice!' There is no doubt that he found it as impossible as we do – to say that word without smiling.

7

The Godly Gourmet

Jesus at the meal table

Jesus was a vegetarian – well almost. There's every reason to assume that Mary cooked and he ate exactly what any other ordinary family had in those days. So in the normal peasant home in which he lived meals would have been very simple, and for financial reasons rarely included meat. For most of the time he, like all the other common people, lived on vegetables, fruit and cereals. Fresh vegetables, onions, leeks, melons, and cucumbers would have been bought by Mary in season, and things like peas, beans, and lentils were also dried and stored. Dates, figs, olives, and grapes, eaten raw in season, and then dried into raisins or pressed into wine, were a regular part of the diet. Jesus ate pomegranates, but as citrus fruits were just beginning to appear in Palestine at his time, it is possible that he occasionally had a grapefruit, lemon, or orange as an unusual 'treat'.

Certainly almonds and pistachio nuts appeared on the menu at the carpenter's house in Nazareth, and they may have done what many families did in that period – keep chickens and poach the eggs in olive oil. Mary would not have used butter very much because of the difficulty of keeping it cool, but she would have made the most of cheese and yoghurt, which were popular foods. The basis of their meals was bread made from barley, or wheat, and when cooked into small flat loaves it was delicious when fresh, but by our standards soon went stale.

Like all housewives, Mary would have used her ingenuity in mixing these ingredients into as appetising a form as possible. Savoury dishes would be flavoured with rock salt from the Dead Sea and perhaps herbs; sweet dishes would include honey from wild bees, or sweetening made from date syrup. Most of the time the food would be boiled together in a stew, or porridge.

Fish was a fairly common item on the menu, particularly the fish from the Lake of Galilee, as we have seen there were at least two eatable sorts, the Musht and the Sprat. In Capernaum they would be eaten by Jesus fresh, but in Nazareth they would more likely have been available to Mary in dried and salted form.

Meat was costly, and only eaten on special occasions like parties, when entertaining guests, or at religious festivals. When available it was boiled mutton or goat meat, for lamb, veal and beef were even more expensive and only the well-off could afford them. The only time in the year when ordinary people saw lamb in front of them was when they treated themselves to roast lamb at the Passover Festival.

In the absence of tea or coffee, wine was the commonest drink. Though water was used for cooking and washing, by the time it had washed down the roofs, run down the gulleys and been stored in the cistern for maybe months, it was not fit to drink before being boiled. Even water specially piped from springs or carried by aqueduct was contaminated, so most people stuck to wine, or milk from the family goat. As the climate in Palestine, Galilee especially, was quite suitable for vine growing, fresh grape-juice was used in season, which was fermented into wine to preserve it for the rest of the year.

In peasant homes breakfast didn't exist, though a snack might be eaten on the way to work or school. The midday meal was simple, perhaps bread, olives and fruit. The big family meal in the evening was usually a vegetable stew; everyone would sit on the floor round the pot and 'dip in', using a piece of bread as a spoon.

But the big difference between their days and ours is the significance of eating together; – it had almost a ritual meaning, they were 'fellowship meals'. The more religious the group was, the more trouble they took to prepare the food, to decide whom to invite, and to purify themselves. The Essenes at Qumram were extremely particular, while the Pharisees were rather more easy-going; they just had to take care always to go to the toilet, to wash themselves in the prescribed manner, to dress in certain vestments, and recite special prayers before sitting down to eat.

In Jewish religion, then and now, the meal has a wide range of religious meanings. All of them signify a 'bonding' between the believer and God, and between believers themselves. In many English households today a special significance is placed on 'Sunday Dinner', and while weekday meals might be taken 'on the run', Sunday is the day on which the family are expected to sit down properly at the right time, and eat together off the best crockery; there is a family importance to the roast beef and Yorkshire pudding. But a Jewish meal, especially on the Sabbath throws this modest English custom into the shade. Theirs is much more heavy with religious and social meaning, and echoing with racial history.

To invite someone to eat with you was more than just being good-natured and hospitable; it was a statement of racial and religious togetherness, acceptance, and solidarity. It was one way in which the Jews emphasized their conviction that they were the 'Chosen People', separate and different. They would not enter the houses of, and certainly not eat with, people who were not 'like us'.

The relationship with someone over the meal-table was a special thing for it meant that from then onwards both host and guest were in a new trusting situation. For either person to betray that trust, either during the meal or afterwards, was a desperately shameful thing to do. This showed itself in the disgrace that fell upon Judas Iscariot. If Mark's Gospel is right and Judas was at the Last Supper, Jesus' words have an added poignancy: 'One of you will betray me – one who is eating with me.' For Judas to betray Jesus was bad, to do it for money was worse, but to do it immediately after sharing a meal with him was despicable.

Several episodes in the ministry of Jesus illustrate this attitude to his meals, and the scandals which arose when he 'broke the rules'.

First Jesus seems to have gone out of his way to eat with the people who would never have been invited to a proper Jewish meal. That is, those whose touch, speech, houses, and food would all render a Jew unclean; tax-collectors, who apart from their unpopularity in working for the occupying power came into continuous contact with Gentiles and were permanently unclean; and sinners, the usual name for the outcasts who didn't bother about these things and were looked down on by the religious people.

What outraged the religious establishment of his day was not that Jesus was degrading himself. After all, why should they worry about that? By acting in this way he were merely sabotaging his own future advancement in religious circles. 'He's done for himself now', they probably said.

No, in fact what upset them was that the Jewish conception of heavenly bliss was to attend the great banquet at the end of time when God would issue the invitations and preside, a picture that runs through both Old and New Testaments. In the Jews' case they thought of it as a glorious Sabbath feast, when all faithful Jews would sit down with Abraham and the prophets and they would eat the great Behemoth and Leviathan and wash them down with wine from the grapes of the Garden of Eden. But they knew that Jesus was well aware of the great vision of the Heavenly Banquet, and that both he and they regarded their meals on this earth as just poor rehearsals for that ideal day.

What Jesus was saying was that when the great Heavenly Banquet comes, in his view the people who would be invited would not be the outwardly religious of his day, but the Gentiles, the tax-collectors and the sinners. Jesus saw them as nearer to God than many, at least, of the pious. Many of the last would be first, and the first last – the 'Chosen People' would not be automatically at the front of the queue to get in. This is what caused the consternation and the uproar, and if we were honest, it would cause equal controversy if said in ecclesiastical circles today!

> You may stand outside and knock on the door crying, 'Lord, open for us,' but the master of the house will say to you 'I do now know where you come from.' You will say 'but we ate and drank in your presence . . .' He will say 'begone everyone of you, you evildoers'.

This saying comes from the book of the 'sayings of Jesus' written before the Gospels, and because no copy of it has ever been discovered and no one knows the author, called Q. What Jesus was saying here is that at the great heavenly banquet the Jews could no longer take it for granted that the guest list would only include Abraham, the patriarchs, prophets, and the Jews, with the Gentiles locked out. The solidarity and fellowship of that cosmic meal, as with his earthly meals, would not be a racial or ritual identity of interest, but one based on a right relationship with God and a fitting way of life. Therefore Jesus' priorities at his own meals would not be the accepted ones of respectable society, but those of God's new guest list. He had no hesitation in eating with people who were regarded by others as prostitutes and crooks, for what came out of their hearts was often purer and better than from others. Instead of being a closed table for the orthodox, it was open to anyone, out went the arrogantly sure, and in came the lost and confused. Among his guests he seems to have been looking not for self-satisfied achievement but for potential – for yearning, for openness, for awareness of need, and a sense of self-disatisfaction.

This is why he had no patience with the ritual rigmarole which had to precede a meal, for it wasn't what you ate or how you ate it that rendered you unclean in God's eyes, but what came out of your heart. This attitude of his was much more than goodwill to downtrodden people, more even than a reaction against the religious practices of his day, it was a considered action that focussed and expressed his whole teaching about the Kingdom of God. He couldn't have given up doing that without giving up his entire preaching ministry.

A classic scandal occurred when he was going through the scorching hot city of Jericho. After making enquiries as to who was likely to respond, a technique which he recommended when training his followers, so would hardly have ignored himself, he spotted and identified the chief tax collector, a notoriously rich man, who had climbed a tree to see him go by. 'Come down Zachaeus, I'll stay with you today', which, of course, meant eating with him. 'The crowd muttered that he'd gone too far!'

Clearly Jesus didn't reject the Jewish concept of meals as

a shared focus of a common identity, but he deliberately reversed that identity, for his judgments were different.

He and his followers were known as good eaters and drinkers, and were criticized for it. They were not tee-totallers like John the Baptist and his followers, or self-denying like many religious sects of the day. 'A glutton and a drunkard', they called him. We know this because Q also included a saying by Jesus which reveals a very human reaction to the criticism. He pictured a crowd of children playing in the market place, 'Let's play weddings', they said, and started to play a flute, but their playmates would not join in and dance. 'All right, then, lets play funerals!' and started to wail, but they wouldn't join in that either. So Jesus goes on to explain: John the Baptist, as an Essene, was puritan to a fault, and you wouldn't follow him. I enjoy my food and drink, and you won't follow me! We can almost see Jesus, holding his hands out, shrugging and saying 'You're impossible!'

The central symbolic act of Christians ever since Jesus has been tied in with a meal, the most significant and far-reaching meal the world has ever seen. So it is an occasion worthy of closer examination.

The preparations for it are interesting because they include a bit of 'undercover' work. It was the rule that the Passover Meal had to be eaten within the walls of the Holy City for all male Jews who lived within a fifteen mile radius, and strongly urged on every other Jew who could come; all inhabitants were instructed to be hospitable to the hundreds of thousands of pilgrims and visitors who crowded the city. There was a tremendous feeling of 'togetherness' as all these people split into groups of ten to twenty to celebrate the feast. They were proud of their nation, proud of their Temple, and proud of their religion and the God who had chosen them for his own. To give some idea of the size of this influx it was said by Josephus

85

that on one occasion a quarter of a million lambs were sacrificed, so if each passover group averaged ten people, this would have made the number in the city and camping on the sloping ground outside the walls about two and a half million people. Even if the figure is exaggerated, it was still an enormous crowd.

Residents in the city were encouraged to lend rooms to visitors, and in return it was the tradition that the skin of the lamb and the earthenware crockery was left behind as a tip. Lambs were bought either in the markets or in the Temple, and in the afternoon before the Passover were taken to the Temple to be inspected by the priests (for they had to be 'without blemish'), killed and dressed, and some of the blood dashed against the altar. The scene in the Temple when so many animals were killed in so short a time must have been so like an abattoir as to fully confirm the Roman condemnation of Jewish Temple religion as 'barbarous'; though it was rather a 'rich' comment coming from Rome. After the service at the Temple the people broke into their groups and made their way, with the carcase of the lamb, to the room they had arranged, to cook and eat the meal.

This acute demand for accommodation meant for Jesus that prior arrangements for a room had to be made, and he knew that he was a 'wanted man'. So he arranged a signal and a password with friends who lived in the city to use their home, and kept it quiet even from his closest disciples.

'Just inside the city gates you will meet a man carrying a water jar; follow him to the house, tell the owner 'the Teacher asks you "Where is the room in which I can eat the passover?"''

Carrying water pots was women's work. A man, even if he was probably a slave, would stick out like a sore thumb among the crowd of women, as a man taking his child to an antenatal clinic is today. Notice that they were not to talk to him, or show any sign of recognition – just to follow.

The ancient tradition is that the place was in the home of John Mark, and the Syrian Orthodox Church of John Mark is now built over what is claimed to be the actual room, which they proudly claim as the 'Mother Church' of all Christendom. If the present room is the same one, or built on the plan of the original, it is surprisingly large.

There is also no record of Jesus attending the Temple service on that afternoon. Did he go well wrapped up hoping to be lost in the crowds? Or did he think it wiser to stay away? We don't know. But we do know that the disciples, dressed in their best clothes, would have been together in a room by nightfall, and heard the Temple trumpet call which indicated that the meal could begin.

The room would be set out simply with low tables, and the guests would recline on mats, with cushions under their elbows. Usually at important meals a slave would be waiting at the door with a towel and basin to wash the dirt of the street off the guests' feet as they arrived. But this was a secret meeting, the disciples probably came in ones and two's so as not to attract attention, and John implies that though the towel and basin were there, the slave was not. As washing guests feet was a menial task, an argument broke out among the disciples as to which of them was the greatest, and conversely who had to wash the feet of the others. The dispute was solved when to the disciples shame, Jesus took the basin and towel and did it himself.

Having arrived there, what sort of meal did they have? There is considerable discussion and argument among scholars as to dates and whether it was a Passover meal or not, because there appears to be some confusion in the timing between John's Gospel, and the other three. As

Jesus was crucified on the Friday before the Passover started at nightfall, and before the Passover lambs were due to be sacrificed in the Temple, some experts think the meal they shared on the Thursday night was either an ordinary meal, a pre-Sabbath meal – the Qiddush, or most interesting of all – the official Passover meal held early and using bread instead of the lamb.

However, cutting through the controversy which some people find fascinating, and others boringly hair-splitting, it seems most likely that it was the Passover meal held early; if it was officially brought forward lamb would be included, if unofficial they would have substituted bread. We can assume this for a significant reason: Jesus seems to have deliberately linked his own death with the classic Jewish 'liberation' meal. Just as Passover harked back to the days when the Jews were preserved by God and escaped from Egypt, so at his last meal he saw himself as the sacrificial lamb of a new escape – the escape and preservation of faithful people from the sin and sterile religious bondage of his own day.

Presuming that this is what happened, what did they eat? If they did indeed have the lamb, this would have been purchased by the household, killed in the Temple, and brought home to be roasted whole on a wooden spit made from pomegranate wood. Any bread would have had to be unleavened.

As far as we can reconstruct how the festival was celebrated at the time of Jesus, the proceedings were in this order:

First there was a blessing of the first cup of wine mixed with water, by Jesus who presided at the feast.

Blessed art thou, O Lord our God, who has created the fruit of the vine. Blessed art thou O Lord our God, King of the universe, who hast chosen us from among all peoples, and exalted us from among all languages, and sanctified us with thy commandments. And thou has given us O Lord, in love, the solemn days for joy, and appointed seasons for gladness: and this is the day of Unleavened Bread, the season of our freedom, a holy convocation, the memorial of our departure from Egypt.

This first cup was then drunk. Afterwards came a hand-washing and an accompanying prayer, though whether Jesus did this is impossible to say in the light of what he said about the custom. The paschal table with the food was then brought forward. On it were the roasted lamb, cut in pieces but with no bones broken, with vegetables like bitter herbs, lettuce, and endives. Jesus then dipped the bitter herbs into a dish of bruised fruits, dates, figs, almonds and raisins mixed with vinegar and spices, a symbol of the clay with which the Jews were forced to make bricks in Egypt. The dipped herbs were then handed round, to symbolize the bitterness of their oppression. Then everyone present sang Psalms 113 and 114, ending with short thanksgivings.

The wine was then passed round again, and Jesus broke the bread with thanksgiving, which in turn was dipped in the dish of fruits. Then the real meal began. They ate the lamb, which may have been followed by unleavened cake as a desert. This was followed by the pouring of a third cup of wine, which because a special benediction was pronounced over it was called 'the cup of blessing', and then the youngest male person attending asked the host what the significance of the feast was. This was the cue to Jesus, or in family situations the father, to tell the classic story of the Jews' escape from Egypt. At the Last Supper who was the youngest – John? A fourth cup of the red wine led to the singing of Psalms 115–118 and was followed by grace after the meal.

On the table would be a full cup of wine, Elijah's Cup, set out in case the prophet should come to announce the Messiah.

As far as we can tell, this is what happened on the night before Good Friday. The passover meal held in Jewish homes today is very similar, though over the years other symbolic touches have been added.

It was after this final meal that Jesus took the things that were to hand, 'he took the cup', it could only have been Elijah's, and the bread, and turned them into a symbol for himself – a symbol that has reverberated down the centuries. While the disciples, confused and worried, were not aware of what was going on, and were lost among the profound undercurrents in that room, Jesus himself was absolutely clear in his mind and precise in what he was doing.

Breaking the bread, he called it 'my body', taking Elijah's cup and passing it round, he called it 'my blood shed for many'. The disciples must have been aware of a special intimacy in this act, done at a moment of particular danger. While Jesus obviously saw something much deeper, regarding himself as the sacrificial lamb in a new Passover, a new covenant between God and his people. They celebrated the old, and then followed it with the start of the new.

Just as Jews were commanded to attend the Passover and remember the deliverance of their ancestors, so Jesus then looked at them and said deliberately, 'when you meet again, do this in remembrance of me'. It was a personal and very human request to his friends, of course, but most Christians think he meant more than that, and cannot escape from the conviction that he knew that he was starting something of historical and universal proportions. Looking back on it, and knowing what we do about what was in his mind and what happened afterwards, it is unbearably moving.

More even than this. Bearing in mind the picture of the Heavenly Banquet, here was Jesus saying 'we'll meet again – there! the next time we share the food and fellowship of the meal table, we shall do it in God's new kingdom, where we'll be on a new and different guestlist.' In this way he made a 'date' with all of his followers, then and since, an engagement to be put on the page at the back of every true believer's diary – the one headed 'Eternity',

'Day after Judgment Day – Banquet.'

8

The Concrete Terrace

Calvary and the empty tomb

If ever there was a perfect example of the topsy-turvy way in which truth can be stranger than fiction it is the case of the Roman concrete terrace. It was a determined attempt of the conquering power to wipe out Christianity which ended in an ingenious twist that would not have disgraced the best short-story writer. The location was that tumultuous place Jerusalem, ironically named 'The Holy City', which historians say has been besieged fifty times, conquered thirty times, and destroyed ten times over. It was there that the massive concrete terrace was built over the little hill upon which Jesus was crucified and over the tomb in which his body was laid.

But before looking at what happened, we should first consider some of the events of the Thursday night and the first Good Friday. We start with the trial, or trials, of Jesus.

When Jesus was arrested he was first brought before the Jewish Council, called the Sanhedrin, comprised of seventy-one Priests and Elders. Taken as a whole the Gospels are rather confusing about what happened; surprisingly the latest Gospel, John's, seems to be the most clear regarding the actual sequence of events. It seems that there were three trials, the first, presided over by Annas the deposed High Priest met at his house, and at night. Both of these actions made the court technically illegal so it had to be an informal investigation at which a decision was reached. This was followed very early the following morning by a full and formal session at the Temple at which the earlier judgment was confirmed. Only after that was Jesus judged before Pilate.

Annas was a High Priest deposed by the Romans, and was the 'power behind the throne'. He operated through his many relations who actually held office, especially his son-in-law Caiaphas, the current High Priest. It seems that Annas held the informal night enquiry, and Caiaphas chaired the formal official trial. Even so, though the Council had complete power in religious matters, it did not have the authority to inflict the death sentence, in these cases it prepared the evidence on which the criminal could be tried a third time before the Roman Governor.

The problem they had was not to decide whether Jesus was guilty, for their plotting with Judas has shown that they were nearly all against him to start with, but to find the legal minimum of two credible witnesses whose evidence against Jesus would be convincing to the higher court. Short of an admission of guilt from the accused, the case would have been thrown out without the first-hand evidence. Various false witnesses were called, but patently would not have stood up to Roman enquiry. The Sanhedrin had the power to compel anyone to attend the court and give evidence, but they couldn't find the witnesses they were looking for.

This is what is behind Peter's denial that he knew Jesus. Naturally, as Jesus' righthand man, he followed all the developments as closely as he dared, creeping into the back of rooms, and following behind the crowds. John gives a memorable glimpse of the trial scene:

Simon Peter was following Jesus with another disciple. That disciple was known to the High Priest, and he went in with Jesus into the courtyard of the High Priest's house. Peter was standing at the door outside. The other disciple, who was known to the High Priest, came out and spoke to the door-keeper, and brought Peter in. The maid-servant who kept the door, said to Peter: 'You are not one of this man's disciples, are you?' He said 'I am not' . . .

So Peter denied knowing Jesus, and did it with increasing emphasis three times. There is much more in Peter's actions than impulsive cowardice. Partly it could have been fear, for though the general mass of the disciples would not have been in particular danger, Peter, as Jesus' closest associate, might well have been. But just as important in Peter's mind, perhaps most important, was that he could have been forced by the Council to give evidence against his master.

The Sanhedrin were trying to prove that Jesus claimed to be the Messiah in order to condemn him for blasphemy. How could Peter, of all people, deny it? For it was Peter who, at Caesarea Philippi, had first recognized him as precisely that! Put in the witness box he would have been in an impossible situation. If he had lied, and said that after all he didn't think Jesus was the Messiah, he would have deserted everything Jesus stood for, and dealt a devastating blow to the rest of the disciples. But if he had bravely stood his ground and repeated his faith in Jesus, his would have been the testimony which condemned his Lord. Peter did the only thing he could think of, denied that he knew him, went outside and broke down in complete frustration and impotence.

The fascinating question is who was the other un-named disciple, the one 'known to the High Priest'? Together with this is the issue of how do we know what went on before Annas, Caiaphas and, later, Pilate? Obviously one or more of Jesus' disciples were present and preserved the dialogue for us to read, which is why the identity of this disciple is so interesting.

Many people have speculated about this. It could have been one of the two members of the Sanhedrin who were known to be sympathetic, Nicodemus, or Joseph of Aramathea, they would certainly have been at the second trial and probably the first, would have recognized Peter at a distance, and both would have been 'known to the High Priest'.

The tradition has been very strong, however, that he was John, the source of the Fourth Gospel, himself. Zebedee, John's father, was a wealthy man, and according to tradition, fished in Galilee, and transported the dried fish to his own shop in Jerusalem. There is a little Crusader church in the old Arab market in Jerusalem now which contains ruins that are supposed to be on the site of Zebedee's Fish Shop. So John, it is argued, delivered the fish to Annas' house, and therefore was known to them, and because he would be well-known to the door-keeper, had entry to the house. It is a homely story and impossible to prove, but if there is truth in it would show that the 'unnamed' disciple could well have been John himself.

Another point is that John was in fact of priestly descent through his relative Elizabeth and his mother Salome. It is possible that John exercised his priestly duties at the Temple occasionally, and was therefore known to the High Priest. An argument in his favour is that the only mention of this episode is in John's Gospel itself, and its the kind of thing that only the people involved would know; as is the little detail that they warmed themselves round a fire of charcoal. Against it is that if Peter could have been called as a witness, so could John who was already known as one, and was just as identifiable from his Galilean accent.

What is significant is that John's account has a rather 'softer' description of Peter's denials; there is no mention of him 'cursing and swearing.' Is it that John doesn't want to 'rub it in'? But Mark, which comes from Peter's preaching, gives all the unsavoury details. Peter was obviously fully prepared to admit the lot.

At the informal pre-trial before Annas, the Temple police who packed the courtyard slapped Jesus' face and generally beat him up, an unthinkable thing in the official trial held later. Interestingly, John's account stops at this point. Did he think it wiser to make himself scarce? But there is no need to assume that Jesus had only one supporter in his hour of trial – there could well have been several whose part in the proceedings is now lost to us, but who remembered and passed on what happened, in particular Joseph of Aramathea. Christians may well owe an immense debt to those early followers of whom we know so little.

The High Priests never did get the two witness they required. In the end Annas had to descend to putting leading questions to the prisoner himself, and finally Jesus in effect admitted that he was the Messiah. If he had not said that, there was no way the charge could have been substantiated. Put together with Jesus' failure to escape when he had every chance, he was clearly a 'volunteer' criminal.

The formal trial was held at the earliest legal hour, the end of the third watch of the night and the start of the last, known as 'cock-crow'. Each watch was marked by a trumpet call from the Temple. The trial seems to have been a perfunctory affair – 'are you the Messiah?' 'Yes.' 'Guilty!' Even so, when Caiaphas sent Jesus on to Pilate, the Roman Governor, he thought it safer to twist the charge from the doubtful one of blasphemy to the more promising one of treason.

In between court appearances Jesus was kept in a cell, and a typical 'bottle' cell has been found after diligent searching for the remains of the High Priest's palace. It is next to an old Roman road, and in the cell are painted crosses which show that it was a venerated place back in the first Christian centuries. The recent church of St Peter in Gallicantu has been built on the site, and on various levels under the church, there is in addition to the usual facilities of a High Priest's house, the inscription 'corban' which meant 'reserved for holy use' on some rooms, scourging blocks, an ancient court-yard, and in the middle of it, the opening to the 'bottle' cell. As soon as a prisoner was condemned he was lowered down the hole into the utter darkness and dirt of the cell, from which there could be no escape.

Interestingly, centuries before, the Prophet Jeremiah suffered the same fate when he was condemned and lowered into a cistern-like cell in the middle of the courtyard, from which he was rescued using a rope of rags.

There are three rather different emphases in the accounts of what happened when Jesus was sent to Pilate, the Roman Governor. Pilate was visiting the city at the Passover time, from his headquarters at Caesarea Maritime, obviously to keep an eye on the crowds who thronged the city. His troops were quartered at the Antonia Fortress, built up against the Temple wall for quick response over a footbridge, but technically outside the city wall so as not to cause offence.

Mark's version is the earliest, and he puts the blame equally on the High Priests and the Romans who actually carried out the execution. We must remember that Mark had no reason for 'going easy' on the Romans, for he was writing for the church in Rome who had just suffered dreadful persecution under Nero, in which both St Peter and St Paul had been martyred. Luke and Matthew, on the other hand, almost exonerate Pilate, accusing the Romans only of weakness and not standing up to the mob. John has a very different account, and shows Pilate taking Jesus up the stairs into his own private apartment, where he is convinced of the sincerity and harmlessness of Jesus, and took a lot of pressure and threats before he was forced to capitulate.

Looking at the records of the trial before Pilate, one is surprised by the amount of time he spent on it. In an area which was a raging sea of bloodshed, and an age when human life was very cheap, from Pilate's point of view the life of one single country Rabbi, orthodox or not, was of such little consequence that it hardly justified so much official time as this one did. It would be foolish to think that the fate of Jesus as a person mattered at all to him. What created the difficulty was what effect his decision would have on the peace of the crowded, volatile city Pilate was held responsible for. He clearly ended up confused, in a moral dilemma, and outmanoeuvred by a people he did not begin to understand. His reputation in Rome was already precarious, so when the howling mob threatened to report him to the Emperor, he gave in and signed the execution warrant.

And so, preceded by a placard, and surrounded by the execution squad, the weakened Jesus, staggering under the weight of his cross, walked the long way round, through the busy market streets crowded with last-minute festival shoppers, to the little hill called Golgotha, just outside the city wall.

On the journey, Jesus could not continue to carry the cross because of his previous scourgings, so the soldiers grabbed a passer-by called Simon, from Cyrene in North

Africa, and ordered him to carry it. A heart-warming sidelight on this is that though Matthew, Mark and Luke tell us this, only Mark says: 'They compelled Simon of Cyrene coming from the country, the father of Alexander and Rufus.' Why did Mark identify the sons by name when no one else did? It has to be that Alexander and Rufus were both known to the church in Rome for which Mark was writing; this is a habit of Mark's which we also see in the case of Bartimaeus. From isolated references we know Simon's sons were involved in the Early Church, so it seems that when the Roman soldiers suddenly picked on a passing stranger to carry the cross, they picked him, and his sons, into the Kingdom of God at the same time.

So they went on to the little spur which jutted out of the side of a worked-out quarry, abandoned because it was stone which the builders had rejected, and there they crucified Jesus in between two common criminals. What he said when hanging on the cross was a microcosm of his entire life. Looking at their content, the words were full of love and concern for his family, his friends, his fellows on the crosses either side, and even for the soldiers who had done it. There is the touching humanity of 'I thirst', and the impenetrable mystery of 'My God, my God, why have you forsaken me?' They are all elements which appear continually throughout his ministry, real humanity showing itself in love for others and revealing a suffering God.

Jesus died surprisingly quickly in the opinion of the expert execution squad, and of Pilate. He did not fight death, or struggle to stay alive – he gave up willingly. For he had known in his innermost soul ever since the temptations that self-giving was the only way to launch the new Kingdom of God. Given the conditions of the time that had to mean the cross. Conspiracy, betrayal, and cowardice had played their part, but in the last analysis the cross was Jesus' deliberate, voluntary and frightening choice. His cry 'it is finished' put an emphatic blood-red full stop at the end of the Jesus of history.

Afterwards, the timid disciple who was also a member of the Jewish Council, Joseph of Aramathea, plucked up his courage, and with the even more nervous Nicodemus to keep him company, asked Pilate for custody of the body. They then put it in the new garden tomb just a few yards away from the crucifixion site. For the time was late, they couldn't leave the body on the cross for days as usually happened, and they had just three hours to deal with it before the Sabbath began. So they unwittingly prepared the scene for the incredible events of the first Easter Sunday.

But now we must return to the story of the concrete terrace. During the forty years or so after these events the site was venerated and remembered by the first Christians in Jerusalem. Herod Agrippa very soon extended the walls of Jerusalem to include the site, so though it was originally 'Without a city wall', it wasn't for long. However, as the private property of Joseph of Aramathea, and a graveyard, it would not have been built on.

The revolt of the Jews against Rome began in AD 66, and the terrifying seige of Jerusalem and its destruction followed. However not being built on, the site of Calvary and the Empty Tomb would not have been affected much. In the sixty five years between AD 70 to AD 135 the city was a shadow of its former self, but repopulation started at once. The Christian community still existed and we have lists of all the bishops of the Jerusalem church in those early days, so it is inconceivable that such an important site would have been lost or forgotten.

Rebellion broke out in an even more violent form in AD 135, and yet again the city was captured and destroyed. The Emperor Hadrian decided to make an end to it once and for all, and rebuilt the entire city on Roman lines, calling it Aelia Capitolina. He banished all Jewish residents on pain of death if they so much as came in sight of it, and included all Jewish Christians as well, for he didn't see any difference between the two. In addition he was adamant that all traces of Jewish and Christian religious sites should be erased forever. Accordingly, on the site of Calvary and the Empty Tomb he constructed a massive concrete terrace, on it, and above Calvary, he erected a statue of Jupiter, and above the Empty Tomb he built a temple to Venus. At the end he must have looked at them with a satisfied feeling that he'd finished with the Jesus People for ever.

However, though the site remained like that for the next two hundred years, it wasn't the end of the story. Jewish Christians were forbidden to enter the city, but Gentile Christians, Greeks and Romans were allowed to stay. The Jerusalem church continued with Gentile members, keeping in touch with Jewish members outside the city, and the new bishops, of whom we have a complete list, were Gentiles too. Pilgrims started to arrive from other Christian churches, and saw Bethlehem, Nazareth, and Galilee, the places they'd read about in the gospels but when they came to Jerusalem, they saw a completely rebuilt city. When taken to see Calvary and the Empty Tomb, they could only look at the Temple and the statue, and their guides were restricted to saying – 'they're under that massive concrete terrace'. So the knowledge of where the place was could be easily handed on from generation to generation – 'it's underneath that great concrete slab'.

Then came a sudden change. In York, Constantine was made the first Roman Emperor to declare Christianity the official religion of the Empire. The depth of his Christian convictions could be regarded as dubious, but this new official status made a loyal ally of Eusebius, the great Christian historian who lived not far away in Caesarea

Maritime at that time, so it is fortunate that we have a first-hand account of what happened next.

The Bishop of Jerusalem, Macarius, showed Constantine the concrete terrace and Eusebius wrote:

> He judged it incumbent upon him to render that blessed locality of our Saviour's resurrection an object of attraction and veneration to all ... This sacred cave certain impious and godless persons had thought to remove entirely from the eyes of men. Accordingly they brought a quantity of earth from a distance with much labour, and covered the entire spot; then having raised this to a moderate height, they paved it with stone, concealing the holy cave beneath this massive mound ...
>
> These engines of deceit were cast down from their proud eminence to the very ground ... and over-thrown. The materials were thrown from the spot as far as possible ... The ground was dug to a considerable depth ... But as soon as the ground beneath the covering of earth appeared, immediately, and contrary to all expectation, the venerable and hallowed monument to our Saviour's resurrection was discovered.

A little way away, still under the terrace, they found also untouched, the little hill of Calvary. So we have the intriguing spectacle of one Roman Emperor undoing the work that one of his predecessors at great expense had done, but also finding an irony that would seem impossible to a writer of fiction. Hadrian's attempt to wipe out this site had precisely the opposite effect, he had preserved it. Left to itself there might have been an outside chance that it would have been forgotten, but his efforts to make people forget it by desecrating it with earth and concrete had indelibly marked where it was.

Constantine wrote to Macarius:

No words can express how good the Saviour has been to us. That the monument of his Holy Passion, hidden for so many years, has now been at last restored to the faithful is indeed a miracle. My greatest wish is, after freeing the site of impious idols, to adorn it with splendid buildings.

In fulfilling this ambition, Constantine then built a massive church over both sites, carving away the hill into which the tomb was cut but preserving the Empty Tomb, just as it was, under a massive dome, and 'squaring off' the rock of Calvary to a great block fourteen feet square by thirty-two feet high.

Since then, like the rest of the city of Jerusalem, the site has undergone many tribulations, but still in the same place one can see the old Crusader Church of the Holy Sepulchre. Digging in the foundations, archaeologists have found remains of the old concrete terrace, underneath the dome is still the Empty Tomb, now heavily ornamented in Russian-Orthodox style, into which one can walk and wonder at the profound and mysterious events that took place there; and up the stairs at one side of the church there are the chapels in which one can see and actually touch the rock upon which, we can be almost certain, the three crosses were planted on that first Good Friday, and where the 'Man who chopped history in half' finished what he had to do.

Naturally the place is the main centre of Christian pilgrimage, services go on continuously, and thousands of Christians visit it every day with varying degrees of awe, devotion and wonderment. Such a feeling about the place is natural, and desirable, providing they don't forget 'the young man dressed in white', for he is crucial to everything that follows.

'And when the sabbath was past Mary Magdalene, and Mary the mother of James, and Salome, brought spices that they might anoint him ... on entering the tomb they saw a young man sitting on the right side, arrayed in a white robe; and they were amazed. And he said "Don't be amazed, you seek Jesus ... he is not here!"'

For the Jesus of History is not there any more, the cross has gone from Calvary, and the tomb is as empty as the young man, sitting on the ledge where the body would have been, said. We are looking at an empty stable from which the horse has long gone, and opening an empty box which contains only the reminiscent scent of what it once held – 'he is not here!' The search for the first century Jesus is a fascinating one, but essentially historic – antiquarian. The man we look for is now gone from the first century into all the ages, and from Palestine to every country. To follow him from this point we have to change our tenses, revise our geography, and rise to a higher reality.

Note:
Outside the Damascus Gate of Jerusalem, next to the Bus Station, there is another tomb of the right period near a vast water cistern, and a rocky outcrop which from a certain direction can look skull-like. This was pronounced by General Gordon a hundred years ago as an alternative site on, it must be said, dubious mystical grounds. The evidence in this chapter shows that it is almost certainly not the right site. Called The Garden Tomb, it has, however, been beautifully landscaped, is an ideal place for prayer, and shows what the Holy Sepulchre site looked like at the time.

9

The Powerful Mosaic

How was he born?

We would hardly think there was any problem about how Jesus came into this world, for we are reminded of it in supermarkets from the end of every August, and in December by strident child carol singers who threaten to sing another one if you don't pay up! But take away the camels, the sheep, and the snow-laden trees, which are really only background scenery anyway, and we are left with an event that is surrounded by strange occurrences; full of paradoxical and profound meanings.

For instance, consider what we could call 'The Case of the Powerful Mosaics'. It started when the army of King Chosroes of Persia, accompanied by chariots and baggage wagons marched south down the hilly spine of northern Palestine, and branching off the main road south of Jerusalem on to a narrow track, trudged towards the hilltop village of Bethlehem. The war had started in AD 614, and Chosroes had invaded the Eastern Roman empire, sweeping with irresistible force through Syria, Galilee, and to the hills of Judaea.

The Jews of Palestine, far from regarding him as an alien invader, welcomed the Persian soldiers as allies against their common enemy – the Christians, and many Jews, eager for revenge against real or imagined insults, joined the Persian host. Messages went out quickly to groups of Jews living outside Palestine to rebel wherever they could, and massacre the Christians who were their townsfolk. The bloodshed begun by Chosroes increased and spread with terrifying barbarism. For every Christian church burned the Christians in Tyre, for example, beheaded a hundred Jewish prisoners and threw their heads over the city wall. Twenty of their churches were burned.

Jerusalem, the largest city, was weakly defended and fell at once, and of the Christians who lived within it 90,000 were slaughtered. The Church of the Holy Sepulchre, built on the site of the Crucifixion and Resurrection, was destroyed along with churches built on the Mount of Olives.

And so the pitiless army moved on to Bethlehem, to the site of the cave in which, so strong tradition had it, Jesus was born. The church they were after was the one built over the cave by Queen Helena, Constantine's mother, and rebuilt and enlarged by the Emperor Justinian in AD 527. It was a very large typically Roman church, built in the style of a Roman town hall; it had two rows of pillars, and was richly lined with marbles and mosaics. But – and this is what proved to be so significant – outside, over the western triple doorways was a great mosaic of the Wise Men, the Magi, carrying their gifts of gold, frankincense and myrrh to the Christ-child.

Arriving in front of the church at the head of his army, King Chosroes found himself put in an unforseen, and uniquely difficult situation. Behind him, his army's blood was up – the Jewish recruits were burning to clear their land of what they regarded as a monstrous perversion of their faith; yet standing in front of him, in costly workmanship and great splendour, was a vast mosaic of his own people, dressed in Persian costume. They were not ordinary Persians either, but Magi, the group of holy and wise men who were the priestly caste in Persia, and were so respected that it was their task to teach and advise all Persian Kings, probably Chosroes himself. How could he destroy this mosaic? The least he owed them was respect and preservation.

There is no historical record of exactly what happened in front of the church on that day. Perhaps Chosroes had a heated debate with his generals and men, it is possible that he was accompanied by some of the Magi themselves and argued it out with them, or maybe just one look was sufficient to enable a decisive king to make up his mind. Whichever way it was, the result was that the Persian army turned in its tracks and went back the way it came without doing what it had come to do, and the church was preserved – by the Magi. The Wise Men whose summing up of the devious King Herod in the Christmas story had made them go home another way, thus protecting the infant Jesus, had again – at least in effigy – preserved the church that celebrated the holy site.

So was kept safe what is probably the oldest church in Christendom still in use today, enabling us in the twentieth century to see and admire it. The powerful mosaic over the great western door has now gone, a victim of delapidation and Muslim laws forbidding restoration, and the interior richness has almost all been replaced by simple colours, and faded paintings. The entrance now is by a stooping side door, made to keep looters out, but the main structure still echoes to the prayers and praises of Christian people; a continuous stream of pilgrims still come to lift the hatches in the wooden floor to expose and admire the last remains of the ancient mosaics; to squeeze down the narrow stairs into the cave and touch the Bethlehem star set in the floor.

The story of what took place in the early years of the seventh century is fairly well documented, but what is the ordinary Christian to make of the original stories themselves – the Wise Men – the Shepherds – and the Virgin Birth? On the one hand these beautiful stories are so embedded in everyone's mind, bringing back memories of childish Christmases, and are associated with so many lovely and sometimes holy sentiments that to criticize or doubt them seems churlish and unfeeling. Yet Christians are not in the business of other-worldly fairy stories and wishful thinking, and if there is real reason to have a hard look at the stories from a historical point of view, we ought as a Christian duty to do so.

Let us turn first to the Wise Men, as they were the ones who saved the Church of the Nativity in Bethlehem. Did it happen as St Matthew's Gospel describes? Were there any Wise Men at the cradle of Jesus? In favour of the accuracy of the story are many details which are certainly true of the period.

The pen portrait of King Herod the Great in the story is absolutely true to life. First he tries to trick the Magi into telling him where the newly-born king is, and then, when this ploy doesn't work, he massacres all the possible children in Bethlehem to make sure that he has disposed of the right one. Flavius Josephus, the Jewish historian of the period, goes into massive detail about Herod, a half-Jewish adventurer who, by flattering the right people, assassinating the wrong ones, and efficiently conducting battles, achieved his position of a Roman client-king. The Romans could not solve the problem of how to govern the country with the consent of the people – nobody could. The community was so split by vicious antagonisms and violence, that it was rapidly sliding into being completely ungovernable.

Herod was the only man who proved strong and unscrupulous enough to hold down that turbulent mix of people, but no one could call what he achieved harmonious peace; Palestine was a bubbling caldron of discontent held down by force and fear. He was a brilliant soldier, plotter, builder, and administrator, and by any standards was a great man, trying to drag a conservative and rebellious people into the 'modern world'.

But at the same time he was a savage tyrant. Herod's blood-curdling life story would provide enough plots for a dozen gory novels or plays. He killed his favourite wife (in his oriental way he had nine), murdered three of his sons, and was so hated by the Jewish people over whom he ruled, that he dare not travel except when surrounded by his army, and dare not live anywhere but in a string of purposely built fortresses. His barbarism ruined the chances of anything good he did being accepted at face value. Even his attempts to feed the hungry during a severe famine were regarded as attempts to curry favour, and his grandiose building schemes as simple illusions of grandeur.

His last order was typical. He felt his life coming to an end, and he knew that the news of his death would be received by all his people, and even by his family, with riotous rejoicing. So he summoned all the leaders of the nation to a conference at his headquarters. He then, in secret, gave orders to his bodyguard that as soon as the last breath had left his body, they were to butcher all the assembled leaders. In this way, said Herod, the news of his death would be greeted with mourning, and not with joy. A horrifying way to wish to be remembered! In fact, his last order was not obeyed, and the Jewish leaders lived to rejoice at the death of an insanely suspicious, devious, clever, treacherous, murderous, and downright evil man. The picture of Herod in the story of the Wise Men is utterly true to what he was like. Neither Josephus or any other secular author of the time mentions Herod's attempt to find the baby in Bethlehem. This is not to say it

109

didn't happen, but the massacre of about fifteen innocent children in an unimportant village wouldn't even deserve a footnote in the infamous catalogue of Herod's crimes.

Of course details like this in the Christmas story cannot prove that it happened as it is written, but at least we know it must have been written down by someone who lived at the time – and who knew what King Herod was really like. We are still left with the question – is the Wise Men story history or a lovely legend?

So let us turn to the other Christmas story, that of the Shepherds as found in St Luke's Gospel. It is completely different from the Wise Men story – which in itself is surprising – how accurate could this one be?

Luke was one of the early disciples, (though not one of the original 'Twelve') and was the close companion and colleague of Paul. Now among Paul's many periods of imprisonment one of the most fully reported is when he was kept in prison in the Roman capital of Palestine, Caesarea Maritime. We know from Luke's account that Paul was there for two years, and that at that point Porcius Festus took over from Felix as governor of the Province. The date when this happened can be pinned down from secular records at AD 59. But what was Luke doing during these two years? His leader was in prison, leaving him marooned outside. Although there was a lively Christian church in Caesarea, for whom in the end he wrote his Gospel, he must have taken the opportunity to continue his research. He was in Palestine, within easy reach of Bethlehem, Nazareth, Galilee, Jerusalem, plus the eye-witnesses of all the significant events Jesus was involved in, and with time on his hands – what else would an interested, intelligent author do? Notice what he says in the introduction to his Gospel.

Since many have set their hands to the task of drawing up an account of the events which were completed amongst us, telling the story just as those who were the original eye-witnesses ... I too made up my mind to carry out a careful investigation of all things from the beginning ... and to write an orderly account of them so that you may have a full and reliable account.

Obviously, a careful and punctilious author like Luke would be careful not to include doubtful, hearsay evidence, and would check everything out as far as he could. Of all the four Gospel writers, Luke comes across as the man with the most modern attitude to what we would call 'evidence'.

When we look at the Christmas story in Luke's Gospel we find a fascinating and unusual development. Immediately after the introduction of the book, Luke suddenly changes his style. From his normal well-written and stylish 'business' Greek, he changes to a classic Hebrew style of Greek for his description of the births of John the Baptist and Jesus, and at the end reverts back to his simple no-nonsense style again. It is as if, in the middle of this chapter I went into the language of Shakespeare and the Book of Common Prayer, full of 'thee's' and 'thou's'. As Luke was writing his Gospel for non-Jewish readers, there seems little point in doing it for them, for they wouldn't have appreciated it. One can hardly imagine him doing it to demonstrate his versatility as a writer – a Gospel isn't that kind of book. So why did he do it?

No one knows the answer to this question, so we must guess. The most reasonable explanation is that Luke was, in effect, saying 'this is a quotation from a Hebrew original'. It is certainly possible that in his travels during those two blank years Luke could have come across many people who could tell him what happened in Bethlehem and Nazareth, perhaps even Mary herself. And also he may have come into possession of the shepherds' story written in Hebrew, a language which it is thought that Luke didn't speak. After translation, he could have felt that it was so beautiful and true as a story, that he included it in his gospel *just as it was*. The reason for leaving it in its old style could have been to make clear to the reader that it was not written by Luke, but included from somewhere else.

This leaves us with the same question we are facing with Matthew's story of the Wise Men. Did Luke expect his readers to accept his account as historical fact, or as a story?

One thing in its favour is the geography of it. When one thinks of Bethlehem one usually imagines it in English terms – a little town, huddled in a valley, and surrounded by a ring of hills upon which the shepherds wander with their flocks. This may be typical of some countries, but not of Palestine, for the truth is the other way round. Bethlehem, like all communities in that troubled land is built on a hill, where you could see an enemy coming, and could not be attacked from above. The towns and villages were, and mostly still are, 'set on a hill where they cannot be hid', and fortified as far as possible against attack. Bethlehem is just such a typical place. The fields where the shepherds kept the sheep are in a saucer-shaped depression just below the village, and along the sides of the fields, cut in the rising ground, are caves. It was in these that the shepherds lived, slept at night, warmed themselves, cooked their food on camp fires, and when necessary, kept the sheep for safety overnight, before setting out in the morning for the best grazing.

Not only were the fields surrounded by caves, but Bethlehem, built on a hill, also had easily dug cellars under the sides or the backs of many of the houses which could be entered from ground level. Indeed many modern houses in hilly areas have these basements today, which are sometimes used as garages for the family car. So in those days the cave or basement was used to stable their equivalent of the car – the donkey, plus maybe, the family cow and a few chickens. Under the Church of the Nativity a whole complex of ancient caves has in fact been excavated.

Thinking of Luke's story of Mary and Joseph not being able to find room at the inn, it is thoroughly true to the geography of the area and the layout of the town that they should be offered shelter either in a shepherd's cave, or a basement stable cave in the town and gratefully accept it – so creating a scene for the birth of Jesus that has delighted painters for centuries.

Yet this intimate knowledge of Bethlehem displayed in the story does not prove that the story is historically accurate, that there actually was a heavenly choir singing to startled shepherds on that first Christmas night. We have to admit the fact that it is impossible to prove.

So let us leave the issue in mid-air for the moment and move on to the third imponderable thing about the coming of Jesus, the Virgin Birth. This always causes great controversy, for it is truly miraculous. Not that one needs to apologize for this, for a Christian who does not believe in miracles isn't a realist. Take away the element of the inexplicable and the miraculous from the Life and Resurrection of Jesus, and we have a 'gutted' gospel which wouldn't save a single soul. We would be perfectly within our rights to say 'given that – what's so difficult about a Virgin Birth?'

But that hasn't stopped Christian and non-Christian scholars examining the alternatives. The first of them is the obvious one, that Jesus was born in a perfectly normal way, as the first child of Mary and Joseph. In favour of this idea is the fact that both Luke and Matthew produce long family trees for Jesus. Though both of these are different,

113

and indeed irreconcilable, they both trace the descent of Jesus through Joseph. What can have been the point of such involved calculations if Joseph wasn't the father of the baby? Mark, the earliest Gospel, doesn't mention any unusual thing about Jesus' birth, and both Matthew and Luke later on in their main narratives refer to Joseph as 'the father of Jesus', and pay no attention to the Virgin Birth mentioned earlier on in their own books.

The experts also point out that the term 'virgin' in Hebrew and Greek speech at the time was not confined to people lacking sexual experience – it was also used of all virtuous young people, married or not. Indeed in a Jewish catacomb in Rome there is an inscription to 'Irene, virgin wife of Clodius'. Another use of the word, particularly in Palestine, was to describe girls before puberty. It is possible that Mary could conceive by Joseph in the first few weeks or months of being capable of child-bearing and while still being regarded in Jewish eyes as a virgin.

From a Christian point of view, this theory would underline the sheer humanity of Jesus, and this would be no bad thing. The fact that Jesus' life speaks to us in ours is strengthened rather than weakened if he was born as normally and naturally as we are.

There have been other theories, much less plausible, put forward which suggest that if he wasn't the natural child of Joseph he must have been fathered by some other human father – that is, that he was what we would call illegitimate! One very early anti-Christian attack suggested an itinerant Roman soldier as the culprit, and even found a name for him! They supported it with Matthew's comment: 'Because Joseph, her husband, was a righteous man and did not want to expose her to public disgrace, he had a mind to divorce her quietly.' Obviously, Joseph thought she'd been unfaithful! Many would regard this possibility as far-fetched and ludicrous, but even if there

114

was any truth in it, the criticism backfires, for far from blasphemously destroying the character of Jesus, in fact it enhances it. The unique character of the Christian God is that he is a suffering God. He is not a remote unfeeling deity to whom our troubles are as of little consequence as an ant's are to us – but one who rejoices over our happiness and weeps over our sorrow. In Jesus he shows himself as a baby born without a home, a wandering preacher who often had nowhere to lay his head, and a criminal who was executed on a trumped-up charge. If he was illegitimate as well – that fits in too!

We human beings are leaned on by the chromosomes and genes we were born with, we are conditioned by the societies we are born into. It fits in with what we now regard as the purposes of God if we see him sending Jesus to fully share our human predicament, and suffer with us in the mess of this world. So even if we can't accept this theory out of honesty, we may even feel that this is a pity!

These, then, are some of the ways that people have interpreted the Christmas stories. To some it may seem like chopping down the family apple tree, but to others the stories gain an added depth through them. Whichever way we look at them, they are light years away from the holly and hangovers of our modern Christmases. The message is far too big to be wrapped in red and green paper, or hidden in a cracker, and that is true whether we go for any of the possibilities outlined above or whether we accept the Christmas stories 'straight'.

Many people quite properly say that 'The stories are in the Bible, so they must be historically true, however miraculous they are.' We may feel strongly that the Christmas stories are an integral part of the New Testament, and that the New Testament witness is strongest when it is taken as it stands. It must be said that down the centuries this is how they have been accepted – as factual history. There need be no controversy, however, between those who accept them as fact and those who don't.

For these stories, factual or not, are parables. No one will doubt that the parables of the Good Samaritan, the Prodigal Son, the Lost Sheep are true. They may, or may not have happened in real life, there may, or may not, have been those particular people in that particular place, but the message the stories communicate is eminently true, and they speak as strongly today to us as they did to those who first heard them.

Whether they are taken as history or parable, the Christmas stories speak just as forcefully, full of meaning and paradox.

The Wise Men, for example, found the new-born king, not in a palace as they expected, but homeless in a stable. They found no splendour but discovered him in a hay-filled manger; not a full-grown strong king, but a fragile and wholly dependent baby; they did not enter into a well-advertised public event, but the secluded intimacy of a mother's relationship with her first-born child. The intriguing message of the Wise Men lies partly in what they found. Everyone in their lives finds a travelling star and tries to follow it – ambition, money, fulfilment – some ideal or other. But if we follow the star the Wise Men chased, we shall be led into surprising places and reach paradoxical, upside-down conclusions. We shall see that if we really want to change things, the best thing is to throw away our missiles, freedom fighters, and selfish economic plans – and substitute a bit of God instead, preferably wrapped up in a baby.

The other significance in the story is in who they were – non-Jews, foreigners, scientists. The marker that Christianity is a world faith and not a Jewish denomination is put down right at the start of Jesus' life. God at

Bethlehem said 'yes' to all our humanity, to our material world, and wishes to redeem our world, as well as save our souls. Now this is either a worldwide truth or it is absurd. That he became flesh, not spirit, and has views about how we should handle our worldliness, is a lit firework under the chair of everyone of whatever culture, kings, kitchen-hands, scientists and all.

The Shepherd's story has equally explosive implications, for shepherds were looked down upon by orthodox religious people, and lived hard, dangerous, and irreligious lives. Even in England, there was until recent times a custom that when a shepherd died his colleagues would put some strands of raw wool on his eyes, so that when he got to the Pearly Gates, St Peter would see it and say 'ah, so you were a shepherd, excused religious duties – come in!'

The underlying theme of this story is brutally clear – Christ was sent above all to ordinary people. The good news of a new regime, a new kingdom, is aimed more at the people who don't go to church than those who do. It is more for the sick and oppressed than the free and healthy; more for the despised than the respectable; more for people like the shepherds – those who are using up all their energy, all their ingenuity battling against life in order to survive until tomorrow – rather than those who find life easy. Far from being tinsel-covered sentimentality, the underlying message of the story of the Shepherds is at the same time revolutionary and comforting.

When we look at the Virgin Birth, it speaks just as forcefully and clearly. Jesus was not just special, he was quite beyond their normal experience. The totality of what he did, what he said, and what he was, made such an impact on the early Christians, that it put Jesus on a level far above any other human being they had ever met. They

117

treasured and passed on every story they could gather about him, including the birth stories. They would think it wholly natural that this amazing person should have an amazing birth and would accept these stories as wholly in keeping with what Jesus was.

Whether these three birth stories are historical fact or parables makes not a scrap of difference. We don't have to make up our minds for the sake of it; if we are uncomfortable about them we can say honestly 'we don't know'. For the question of whether they are history or parable isn't the important one. 'What think ye of Christ?' is what really matters.

Far from being the peculiar, and ignored, printing on chapel poster-boards, it is the crux of the whole issue. This is why we have to consider the question of his birth at the end of his life, and not where one would naturally suppose, at the beginning. Was Jesus a good man who talked about truth, or was he Truth? Did he come to talk about salvation, or was he the Saviour?

That is the underlying challenge of all the Christmas stories, and it is the decision that every one has to make, and no one else can make it for us. God has something like 5,000 million children in this world, but he hasn't any grand-children at all! In the end our relationship to God is a one-to-one relationship that nobody can steal from us, and nobody can create for us. Like many others before him, an American, Lew Wallace spent six years in an impartial investigation of the truth or falsity of Jesus. In the end he, like so many of them, said 'I have come to the deliberate conclusion that Jesus Christ is the Messiah of the Jews, the Saviour of the world, and of me.'

Many millions of people, clever and stupid, wise and foolish, rich and poor, have come to the same conclusion. They have accepted what the Christmas stories actually

118

say, regardless of how they interpret them as history. They have found that Jesus was more than a good man, or a profound teacher, he was unique; the man who chopped history in half has also cut through their mental blocks and emotional prejudices, and opened them up to God.

10

The Dangerous Search

The Christ of faith

Up to now this has been a thoroughly dangerous book. Our search for what Jesus was really like has resulted in a clearer picture than the usual Sunday School portrait, and given glimpses of a much more 'real' person than pious devotions usually allow. We are at the stage when we can throw away the image one writer caustically described as 'a frail and kindly visionary with no knowledge of human nature as it really is, or an amiable young preacher with a special talent for touching the hearts of women's meetings'. We do not see a phantom or an angel; instead, a much grittier, tougher, rounded, unsentimental character begins to appear – but doesn't quite.

For this we must be overwhelmingly grateful. For the peril in looking for the Jesus of history, though it may possibly lie in the search, assuredly does lie in the finding. If we ever succeeded in bringing him completely into focus, we would open the door to a fascinating and irresistible stairway down to hell. For we should find ourselves worshipping a God two thousand years out of date, and trying to impose a particular ancient Middle-Eastern culture on a world which would reject every transplant we tried to make.

Suppose he had not disappeared from human sight;

consider the alternative. If we try to imagine that he continued to live down the centuries in human form, ageless and eternal, what would we have? A super-Pope? With a shudder we can envisage the appalling prospect of the great King of Kings travelling the world surrounded by rituals, bureaucrats, and television cameras, utterly isolated from real people. He would have no chance of even meeting everyone in the world, let alone really knowing them, for his appearances would be in front of huge crowds and we should sell the front seats to the rich, for charity of course.

This would be as excruciating to us as to him. But on the other hand, suppose we imagine Jesus rebelling at all this and wandering in disguise through the ages doing what he could, where he could. How many times would he have been persecuted, discriminated against, assassinated, and in modern ways crucified yet again? Would eternal replays of his first life's experiences advance us any further from the first Good Friday?

Suppose, on the other hand, new techniques enabled us to find out everything about his first-century life. We would turn the relics and remains of his earthly existence into objects of piety. For example, if someone digging on Glastonbury Tor actually found the Holy Grail – the chalice used at the Last Supper – with irrefutable evidence that it was genuine, one doesn't have to be overly cynical to know what we would do. We would lavish on it the veneration we owe to the person who used it; we would ornament it at great expense and ask the poor to contribute; we would give it the attention and loving care that we ought to be spending on the hungry, thirsty, the homeless and the prisoner. We can only be thankful that it has never happened. Looked at realistically, the only objects from his life which might possibly be more help than hindrance would be the towel and the basin from that Last Supper.

121

A faith that needs to be bolstered by proofs of Jesus' human existence has the mark of doubting Thomas about it, and a devotion that centres on something physical is halfway to superstition and idolatry.

The cry from the cross, 'it is finished', was right – there really was nothing else Jesus could have done; there was no future for the historical Jesus as such, and he knew it. For he was fully aware that the next stage had to be something very different, a widening into the vastnesses of the God he called 'father'. The Jesus of History had to be transformed into the Christ of Faith.

Napoleon, a man not unacquainted with fame, put the contrast very well:

Alexander, Caesar, Charlemagne, and I have founded great empires; but upon what do these great creations depend? Upon force. Jesus has founded his empire upon love and to this day millions would die for him ... I have inspired multitudes with such devotion that they would have died for me, but to do this it was necessary that I should be visibly present, with the electric influence of my looks, of my voice ... Christ alone has succeeded in so raising the mind of man towards the Unseen that it become insensible to the barriers of time and space.

This is why the Risen Jesus on the first Easter Morning said to Mary, 'Don't hold on to me.' It is a message spoken to every curious believer. His own features had to dissolve into the faces of every ordinary man and woman, his voice had to reflect its cadences in the words of every preacher, the look in his eyes had to be seen coming from compassionate nurses, his hands and feet had to be recognizable in the Home Help and the Meals on Wheels ladies. It had to be that way, any other was a nostalgic dead end.

There is another more sophisticated trap lying in wait,

for it is terribly easy for the sincere follower to try to mimic Jesus in present-day life, saying, 'What would Jesus have done in this situation?' What Jesus did and said in first-century Galilee was a mixture of truths local and universal, domestic and eternal, and was addressed to the people he was talking to in their situation. To try to copy in a vastly different time and place the things he did then can lead to a literalism which denies the spirit of what he was. It is far better to ask not 'What would Jesus have done?' but 'What does Jesus *now* want me to do?' Not 'I'll try to copy Jesus in this situation,' but 'I *am* Jesus here.' The timely must become timeless, the ancient ageless.

There is an old funeral hymn which begins:

> Rejoice for our brother deceased,
> Our loss is his infinite gain.
> A soul out of prison released,
> And freed from its bodily chain.

The Jesus the disciples knew had to have his bonds broken, he had to be released from the chains of his century, and be freed to save the world. After the first traumatic days the first Christians knew that, and saw the dangers of hanging on to his humanity too much. John records Jesus saying these things to his friends: 'Because I have said these things to you, sorrow has filled your heart. But I tell you the truth, it is expedient for you that I go away.' For the disciples, used to walking with him in the cornfields, discussing with him at mealtimes, leaning on him, relying on him, this must have been a difficult adjustment. They found it hard to lose sight of the leader they recognized, to hear no longer the voice they knew – they were bewildered and grief-stricken people. Even with the physical presence of Jesus with them they had not found it easy, when the crisis came they all ran away. But as William Temple once said, 'The task of the teacher is to prepare the pupil for the time of separation, which must come . . . it is not only that this time must come, it is a good thing that it should come.'

In fact the disciples did much better after the Resurrection than before. They were more courageous, more daring, more faithful to the Christ of Faith than ever they had been for the Jesus of History. They soon saw that to wish for the earthly Jesus back again would be a retrograde step, the transformation was indeed 'expedient' for them. For as before they could not take Jesus everywhere with them, now 'in the spirit' they could. Whereas before they could not all share their doubts and difficulties with him all at once, now 'in the spirit' they could. When as before his culture as a Galilean Jew created barriers, now 'in the spirit' it didn't.

This is why the writers composed Gospels, not biographies. They could see that however fascinating the natural curiosity about the earthly Jesus was, it hid dreadful traps. There was a crying need in the Early Church for some written record of the message Jesus preached, the things he did, the death he died, and the way he rose. How were they to supply this demand while avoiding the pitfalls?

Mark, for instance, was writing under the stress of the persecution by Nero. There was no knowing when there would be a dreaded knock on the door, and the last ones who knew what Jesus had done would be dragged away, as Peter and Paul had been, and turned into gory amusements for the depraved court. Converts were coming into the church as a result of their preaching, and they wanted to know more about the Saviour who had touched them.

Also books sometimes get into places where preachers can't, and would be read by the literate part of the population who wouldn't be seen having anything to do with the looked-down-upon Early Church. Then, too, new preachers were seeking in permanent form the accurate background of the faith which had fired them. There was an evangelistic need waiting to be filled, so something had to be written down, but in what form?

A biography would have been possible, as it was a well-known form of literature in those days. But Mark did not write one. The early Christian writer Justin Martyr described his story as 'memoirs', the nearest pagan type of book he could think of. In fact Mark wrote the first of a unique form of literature – a Gospel. There is not enough personal detail about Jesus in it to make it a biography, and not enough about Mark to be a memoir. Why, in his aim to present Jesus as the Living Lord, did he do it this way? It seems that one factor in his mind, perhaps the predominant one, was that a biography of Jesus would have focussed the attention too strongly on the Jesus of History instead of on the Christ of Faith. He felt so emphatically that it shouldn't be a memoir either that he cut out references to himself and wrote it anonymously.

It was inevitable and natural that Mark decided to include every story about Jesus that he thought was important to the life and mission of his own church in Rome. He saw the Living Christ within the living Christian community and the new book could not be divorced from it. So the choice of material and the way it was arranged was, as it had to be, a reflection of his own local understanding of what the important themes of the faith were.

Mark was followed by Luke, and the authors of Matthew and John, who, spurred on by their own situations, copied his new Gospel format, and shared his convictions on these matters. They, too, reflected their own local needs and understandings, left out the incidental details about Jesus, and refused to autograph their manuscripts. For them too, the Christ of Faith had overtaken and overshadowed the Jesus they may have known.

Paul's warning about delving too much into the human Jesus is contained in the second letter he wrote to the church in Corinth: 'From now on we regard no one from a worldly point of view. Though we once appreciated Christ by what he was in the flesh, we do so no longer. Therefore, if anyone is in Christ he is a new creation.' There is considerable discussion about this statement which seems to imply that Paul actually met Jesus, did he or not? It is, of course, possible that Paul, studying under Gamaliel in Jerusalem, could have done. But there's no need to make up our minds because what Paul is saying is that whatever he may or may not have known of Jesus, the Christ of Faith who appeared to him on the Damascus Road overwhelmed that previous knowledge. We should not cling to the details of his personal life, although they were done for our salvation, but pass over them quickly in order to reach Christ himself. The Jesus of History was too worldly to be timeless, too localized to be universal, and it does no good to search for him in the past because, as the 'young man in white' said, he is no longer there.

Paul then goes on to the great new concept of faithful people being 'in Christ'. Of course, as we have seen, the Christ of Faith can in spirit be 'in us', strengthening, guiding, comforting. But Paul turns this idea on its head, we can be 'in Christ'; the whole believing Christian community is his body, and in every place and time lives, loves, suffers, and rises with him. It is a New Creation, and everyone who is part of it becomes new.

So the problem with Christ is not any longer to pin him down in the past, but to chase his shadow into the future. As Helmut Thielicke put it:

He is already far out in front of every age that tries to come to grips with him, and more up to date than any 'modern' age which feels itself superior to all that has gone before. He is always the newest and most up-to-the minute on this old-fashioned earth, the living one on the field of dead bones. For he said 'Behold I am with you always, even unto the end of the world.'

For nearly twenty years a unit at a famous university has been studying the religious experiences of ordinary people, categorizing and examining the nature of them. They have found that a surprising number of people, many not committed to any church, have had what they would describe as a 'religious experience' – a sense of presence, of enhanced life. There is a vast proportion of people who have a broadly sympathetic attitude to churchy things, partly as an 'afterglow' from a more churchgoing age no doubt, but also because they know that there is a spiritual dimension to life. It may be nameless, impossible to define or explain, but somewhere and sometime they have been touched by something good and 'other'.

For example, John Rowntree in 1874 was on the threshold of a great personal mission when he was told the devastating news that within a few years he would be totally blind. Dazed and overwhelmed he staggered from the doctor's surgery into the street, where he stood in silence – and suddenly felt a love wrapping him round like a visible cloak, and a joy, like he had never known before, filled him.

Many can mirror Isaac Pennington's words when he experienced the same thing: 'This is he: there is no other; this is he whom I have waited for and sought after from my childhood, who was always near me ... but I knew him not distinctly.' In many cases it does not lead to anything except a mystified wondering, and perhaps wandering. But call that experience the finger of Christ touching us, and beckoning to us to follow, and that experience suddenly has direction and purpose. Instead of aimless wandering, we find ourselves on a paper-chase over a roller-coaster, faced with breathless demands, and betting with life and death stakes. Being in Christ has always been like that. He has always asked for more than in our own strength we can give, always demanded what is impossible without him. Which is why being 'In Christ' has to go with Christ being 'in us'.

There are some people who wish they they had the eloquence to persuade a materialistic and careless age to look to Christ. There are others who wish that they had such charismatic and loving personalities that they could fill churches by their winsomeness. But as we grow older we realise that the best gift we can wish for others, is not to hear the most eloquent sermon, or be won over by the most attractive personality, but that in the middle of an ordinary day and ordinary concerns, they may catch a glimpse of the grace of eternal love – that they may feel the touch of the finger of Christ, and recognize whose it is.

How do we put a name to these experiences of profound mystery? How can we identify who it is who has stopped us dead, short-circuited our materialism, and made our flesh tingle?

We know that it is Christ because of the flesh and blood that lies behind it – because of the *Jesus* of it. This is why the search for the fascinating character who took a divine cleaver to human history and divided BC from AD is so important.

References

Introduction

He comes to us – Albert Schweitzer, *The Quest of the Historical Jesus*, A. & C. Black 1954, p.401.

1   The Divine One-Off

So Joseph woke – Matt. 1. 25.
Description of Jesus – *The Rise and Influence of Rationalism in Europe* quoted in W. Moodie (ed.) *Tools for Teachers*, Elliot Stock 1898.
He had no beauty – Isa. 53. 2–3.
Woman of Samaria – John 4. 1–31.
They brought little children – Mark 10. 13.
The house – Mark 9. 33.
He took a child – Mark 9. 36.
They stepped back – John 18. 6.
Zacchaeus short? – Luke 19. 3.
They rose up and hustled – Luke 4. 30.
The house was beset – John Wesley's Journal. July 4 1745.
Invective against Pharisees – Matt. 23.
White-washed tombs – Matt. 23. 27.
Tunic with no seam – John 19. 24.
Glutton and drunkard – Luke 7. 34.

2   Joseph and Sons' Biggest Order

Revolt of Sepphoris – *The Life of Flavius Josephus*, section 67.
Anything good from Nazareth – John 1. 46.
Children's first Psalms – Psalms 114 and 121.
First-born males – Ex. 13. 12; Num. 18. 15.
Offering of the Poor – Luke 2. 24.

Child Jesus lost – Luke 2. 41–52.
Is this not the carpenter? – Mark 6. 3.

3 A Man of his Time

You hypocrites – Mark 7. 6–8.
Brood of vipers – Matt 12. 34.
Whose sandals – Matt. 3. 11.
The greatest man – Luke 7. 28.
Baptism in Jordan – Matt. 3. 13–17.
The coin in the fish – Matt. 17. 27.
Fish and serpent – Matt. 7. 10.
That fox – Luke 13. 32.

4 The Shameful Stones

Call of Matthew – Matt. 9. 9.
Eating with tax-collectors – Matt. 9. 10.
Centurion's servant – Luke 7. 2ff.
Jairus' daughter – Luke 7. 1–10.
The hard word – John 6. 50–66.

5 Parlez-Vous Aramaic?

Talitha Koum – Mark 5. 41.
Ephphatha – Mark 7. 34.
Abba – Mark 14. 36.
Eloi, Eloi – Mark 15. 34.
Syrophoenician woman – Mark 7. 24–30; Matt. 15. 21–28.
The naked maniac – Mark 5. 1–20; Matt. 8. 23–24; Luke 8 26–39.
The unclean pig – Lev. 11. 8.
There were some Greeks – John 12. 20.
Don't speak to us in Hebrew: – II Kings 18. 26.
Jesus in the Synagogue – Luke 4. 16.
The placard – Mark 15. 26; Matt. 27. 37; Luke 23. 38; John 19. 19–20.

6 The Happy Breeze

Trumpets in almsgiving – Matt. 6. 2.
Looking miserable – Matt. 6. 16.
The yoke – Isa. 58. 6–9; Jer. 28. 10–12; Matt. 11. 29.
The harlots go into the kingdom – Matt. 21. 31.
The splinter and beam – Matt. 7. 3; Luke 6. 41.
The camel and gnat – Matt. 23. 24.
ᵣ ᵗe dead bury the dead – Matt. 8. 22; Luke 9. 60.
ᵗefore swine – Matt. 7. 6.
vorry – Matt. 6. 25ff.

Simon nicknamed Peter – Mark 3. 16; Matt. 16. 18; Luke 6. 14.
Rewarded a hundred times – Mark 10. 30.
Mock admiration – Mark 7. 9.
Old and new wine – Luke 5. 38.
Unjust steward – Luke 16. 9–16.
Steal the bank – E. Trueblood, *The Humour of Christ*, Harper & Row 1964, p.101.
The kings of the Gentiles – Luke 22. 25.
Syrophoenician woman – Mark 7. 24ff; Matt. 15. 21ff.

7   *The Godly Gourmet*

One will betray me – Mark 14. 20.
I do not know you – Luke 13. 26.
Making enquiries – Matt. 10. 11.
Zacchaeus – Luke 19. 1–10.
Playing weddings and funerals – Luke 7. 31–34.
The Passover room – Luke 12. 10.
'My body, my blood – Mark 14. 22–24.
Do it in remembrance – Luke 22. 19–20, I Cor. 11. 23–25.
The heavenly banquet – Mark 14. 25.

8   *The Concrete Terrace*

Simon Peter at the door – John 18. 15.
John a priest – Luke 1. 5.
Peter's swearing – Mark 14. 71; Matt. 26. 74.
False witnesses – Mark 14. 56.
Jesus' confessions – Mark 14. 62; Mark 15. 2.
The formal trial – Mark 15. 1; Matt. 27. 1.
Bottle cell – Jer. 38. 6.
Jesus before Pilate – Mark 15. 1–5; Matt. 27. 11–14; Luke 23. 1–4; John 18. 28–38.
Simon of Cyrene – Mark 15. 21; Matt. 27. 32; Luke 23. 26.
Bartimaeus – Mark 10. 46.
It is finished – John 19. 30.
Discovery of the Holy Sepulchre – 'Life of Constantine', Eusebius, *Ecclesiastical History* III. 25.
Asking for the body – Mark 15. 43; John 19. 38–39.
The young man in white – Mark 16. 5.

9   *The Powerful Mosaic*

The story of the Wise Men – Matt. 2. 1–12.
The story of the Shepherds – Luke 2. 8–20.
Luke's introduction – Luke 1. 1–4.

Jesus' family trees – Matt. 1. 1–17; Luke 3. 23–38.
Virgin Birth – Matt. 1. 18–25.

10   The Dangerous Search

It is expedient that I go away – John 16. 6.
A new creation – II Cor. 5. 16.
Far out in front of every age – H. Thielike, *How Modern Should Theology Be?*, Fontana 1969, p.20.